P9-EGN-081

TRAVELERS' TALES

her fork
in the road

women celebrate food and travel

TRAVELERS' TALES

her fork
in the road

women celebrate food and travel

Edited by
LISA BACH

Series Editors
JAMES O'REILLY AND LARRY HABEGGER

TRAVELERS' TALES
SAN FRANCISCO

Art Direction: Michele Wetherbee
Cover Art: Donna Ingemanson
Interior design: Kathryn Heflin and Susan Bailey
Page layout: Patty Holden, using the fonts Bembo and Boulevard

Distributed by: Publishers Group West, 1700 Fourth Street, Berkeley, California 94710.

Library of Congress Cataloging-in-Publication Data

Her fork in the road: women celebrate food and travel/edited by Lisa Bach.
    p. cm.
  ISBN 1-885211-71-6
   1. Food—Anecdotes. 2. Travel—Anecdotes. I. Bach, Lisa, 1968–

TX357 .H4637 2001
641.3'0082—dc21

                    2001034739

First Edition
Printed in the United States of America
10 9 8 7 6 5 4 3 2 1

One cannot think well, love well, sleep well,
if one has not dined well.

—VIRGINIA WOOLF, *A Room of One's Own*

Table of Contents

Part Five
ONE LAST BITE

Introduction: A Taste of What's to Come

The table was set with a gorgeous linen cloth, Mom's fine china, and Grandmother's heirloom silver. Candles provided the only light in the dining room, and beautiful serving dishes were strategically placed, overflowing with treats I had savored while in Italy: spiced cracked green olives, a golden Tuscan olive oil that had captured the sun, and *grissini torinesi*, Italian breadsticks. The small plates arranged with a classic French niçoise salad of baby lettuces, green beans, petite potatoes, egg wedges, olives, and tuna in a delicate vinaigrette, reminded me of the shopping I'd done while strolling on the rue Moufftard in Paris. Around the table, spoons grew heavy with my version of *aardapple soep*, a creamy Dutch potato soup that I had sampled in a convent in a small town outside Utrecht. As I ladled the mushroom stroganoff onto a bed of soft noodles, I recalled the weeks I had spent in Yugoslavia eating nothing but bread and cheese, and the elation I had felt on my first day in Munich when I stumbled upon a vegetarian restaurant, where the stroganoff was a staple. When protests arose from my family—"We're too full!"—I simply brought out something no one could refuse, homemade crepes stuffed with sliced bananas and a thin layer of Nutella. The *coup de grâce* was the one item I purchased in every country I visited: Kindereggs, chocolate eggs in whose centers small gifts were concealed. One for each guest. The meal was complete.

This dinner was my attempt to share with my family a life-changing experience I'd had: a college semester spent traveling in Europe. When I returned home, I thought, I can't just show them my photos and all the bits of paper, tiny French-fry forks, and other miscellaneous souvenirs I collected. So I decided to prepare a meal for them as a way to share my journey, using each dish to tell a different part of my story. The fare I had savored abroad reminded me—and informed my family about—the wonderful places I had visited, and although the dishes did not go together to form an easily digestible meal, they proved to be the best way for me to articulate my many travel experiences. As I prepared, cooked, and savored the meal with my friends and family, they could smell, taste, and delight in my journey, as I knew I always would.

"What was the most memorable and the worst thing you ate while you were there?"

I can't help myself. Food is invariably the first thing I inquire about. Of course, I then always ask about the rest of the trip, but for me the most interesting and revealing conversations about travel often begin with one's gastronomical adventures. Once you get someone talking about her remarkable feasts and favorite fare abroad, you are sure to also hear about the stomach-turning meal and other tales of disastrous dining.

The connection between food and travel is an organic one, for many reasons. Food is an immediate memory trigger: one bite and in an instant you return to that balmy evening spent on a beach in Puerto Vallarta, where you and your lover dined on succulent grilled prawns, homemade tortillas, and a fresh guacamole made only seconds before from a tidy pile of tomatoes, peppers, lemon, and avocado. One evening you're standing in your kitchen, preparing dinner for your family, and just as you add that last pinch of ground cumin to the pot, you remember your astonishment at the rich color of the various spices available at the marketplace in India. Or perhaps you feel a hunger pang and it reminds you of when all the banks were closed in Amsterdam and you only had enough guilders in your pocket to buy a cone of *pommes frites*. It wasn't much of a meal, but it was comforting and satiated you for the evening.

Food is also a window into the cultures and countries we visit: as we go to local restaurants, share meals prepared in the homes of newfound friends, adventure through market stalls with traveling companions, and wonder at the strangeness and sensuousness of new cuisine, we learn directly—through our senses—what it means to travel and experience the world. *Her Fork in the Road* reflects this profound relationship between travel and food. I've prepared a tasty menu of stories by women about food and travel, so that you too can share the delight, passion, and adventure they experienced while sampling the world's culinary bounty. In order to bring together these wonderful stories, I explored the contemporary landscape of food and travel literature, and also read hundreds of stories that were submitted directly to me for consideration. This is clearly a topic that resonates with women writers and travelers, and here you'll find classics from modern culinary literature by M.F.K. Fisher, Elizabeth David, Ruth Reichl, Frances Mayes, Laurie Colwin, and others, as well as many new voices that have never been published before.

But why a book about *women*, food, and travel? Women have a unique relationship with food, one that revolves around issues of self, family, and society. We're often defined by how thin or fat we are, or whether we're able to be home every evening to cook a decent meal for our families. Some women struggle with food disorders throughout their lives, often waging a fierce life-and-death battle. And the kitchen has always been women's territory, women's sacred space in which to gather, chat, and prepare sustenance for the family. And women also have a distinctive way of traveling that lends itself to culinary adventures, whether they are invited into a local woman's kitchen, attend a cooking school, or dissect a recipe in a foreign restaurant to re-create at home. Women's connection to food is both personal and communal, positive and negative, troubled and life-affirming.

Perhaps this is why so many women love "food porn," whether it's films such as *Chocolat, Babette's Feast,* and *Like Water for Chocolate*, with their lingering shots of food being arranged, dished up, and delighted in, or food confessionals such as Ruth Reichl's *Comfort Me with Apples*, Isabel Allende's *Aphrodite*, and anything written by the late M.F.K. Fisher.

Food can be as sensual and comforting as a lover, as the stories in this book reveal. A meal can slowly seduce you with each course, as M.F.K. Fisher experiences in a long lunch she is served by an anxious waitress in a restaurant she stumbles upon on her walk to Avallon. How one eats a meal can also be extremely sensuous, as Ruth Reichl discovers in "A Second Helping" while watching her friend receive a lesson from an attractive Tunisian man in how to eat delicate grains of couscous with only the tips of her fingers. And in "On Pleasures Oral" Linda Watanabe McFerrin and her husband sit back and watch as a Venetian restaurant owner spends the evening trying to seduce their friend with wine, pasta, and the promise of a secret recipe.

Have you ever taken a bite of something and had to pause because it tasted otherworldly? Tamara Holt has a mystical experience while traveling in Greece, where a woman walks "the streets like a missionary of taste, offering sacraments to the unenlightened…communicating without words, through the language of food." She accepts the edible gift and is left standing in the street alone, pondering this strange encounter. And Dervla Murphy attends a going-away party in "Purifying Spirits" where she imbibes local potent spirits, enters into an altered state, and the next morning is left exorcising her "personal Goddess of Destruction." The stories in *Her Fork in the Road* explore the spiritual and mystical nature of food.

The writers gathered here also reveal the essential role that sharing food together plays in creating and cementing family bonds. Whether we are gathering for the nightly meal at home or sharing meals while traveling abroad, my family has always used food as a way to come together. On vacation, we plan our days around mealtime. At breakfast, we talk about lunch. During lunch, we negotiate where to have dinner. And at dinner, we discuss the pleasures of the day, including what we consumed. Many families eat and travel together, and in Libby Lubin's "Please Pass the Snails, Mom" we find surprising gifts when parents travel with their children and encourage them to try everything—including the unusual items on the menu.

Food also enables women to discover things about themselves—and to create lasting bonds with other women they meet in their travels. During a home-stay Lynne Vance, in "Sampling *La Vie Provençale*," connects with her French hostess through her realization that a Frenchwoman's life typically consists of the same everyday tasks that American wives and mothers must perform: shopping, cleaning, and doing grown children's laundry even after they've moved away from home. While in France, she savors the *au naturel* code of shopping for and cooking with only the freshest ingredients, and line-drying laundry to soak in the "fruity, herbal bouquet" of her home-stay family's garden. In "A War with Grandma," Ashley Palmer declares a silent battle when her adoptive Japanese grandmother decides to test her palate with a variety of snacks. The battle binds them together, and a winner is declared only when Ashley decides to make her own sweet offensive move. When a woman invites you into her home and kitchen, she gives you an invaluable opportunity, whether it's to learn how to prepare a local dish or to gain her lasting friendship.

Travel also pushes you to be adventurous, daring, or hungry enough to try just about anything. When you visit abroad, it's sometimes hard to maintain your usual dietary habits, as Stephanie Elizondo Griest discovered during her year in China. In "The Culinary Revolution," after being a vegetarian for years, she quickly decides to expand her gastronomical horizons to include chicken feet, dried beef, and a taste of something that ensures her a carnivorous future.

Not all stories about food and travel are easy to swallow. Sometimes food prompts a personal struggle, a painful memory, or a cultural challenge to overcome. In Michelle Hamilton's story "The Long Road," she reveals her battle with an eating disorder that is forced to the surface on a bike ride across the United States. This extended journey allows Michelle to begin to vanquish her disorder, an enemy since high school, as she realizes that she needs food to continue her journey eastward and to survive. In Laura Harger's "Blue Crabs," her mother is too sick to eat, yet she finds the strength to teach Laura the secrets of cracking open and the joys of eating Chesapeake blue crabs. In sharing this last meal together, Laura finds something to remember her mother by.

Throughout *Her Fork in the Road*, as the gastronomic travelers in this collection attest, food is both a window to the world and a lens through which we examine other people and ourselves. I hope that you, too, are open to discovering the traveling gourmet in yourself. I often think of my defining moment as a roaming gastronome, when I realized that food was indeed the aspect of travel that gave me the most pleasure and exhilaration. After a long day spent walking through Bruges, Belgium, I was exhausted, but knew I wanted to splurge on a typical meal of mussels and *pommes frites*. I walked all along the central town square, but it was clear that my best bet was someplace off the beaten track. I wandered from restaurant to restaurant, peering in and reading the menus. Finally, I turned down a street and heard soulful jazz flowing out of the doors of a candlelit entryway. I entered the bar and walked upstairs to the restaurant, where I was seated in the corner. I'd already been on the road for six weeks, so by this point I felt comfortable eating alone. I ordered a local Trappist Monk beer and waited for my highly anticipated dinner. The waiter carried to my table a large black pot filled with mussels drenched in a sauce of leeks, butter, and cream, accompanied by a plate of *pommes frites*. I just about died. Halfway through my meal, with a mound of empty shells growing fast in front of me, the German couple at the table next to mine interrupted and asked, "Would you like us to take a picture? We've never seen anyone so excited about a meal before." I still have that picture—it's embarrassing to admit, but I'm glowing.

Her Fork in the Road is a tribute to such moments, the times when you stop to savor your journey. My main desire in collecting the stories you are about to read is to give you a memorable taste of women celebrating food and travel. I hope this book accomplishes just that, and makes you hungry—both to travel, and for something to eat.

—LISA BACH

PART ONE

ESSENCE OF FOOD

M . F . K . F I S H E R

I Was Really Very Hungry

*Years ago, a waitress seduced a gourmand
with an exquisite meal.*

ONCE I MET A YOUNG SERVANT IN NORTHERN BURGUNDY WHO
was almost frighteningly fanatical about food, like a medieval
woman possessed by a devil. Her obsession engulfed even my
appreciation of the dishes she served, until I grew uncomfortable.

It was the off season at the old mill which a Parisian chef had
bought and turned into one of France's most famous restaurants,
and my mad waitress was the only servant. In spite of that she was
neatly uniformed and showed no surprise at my unannounced
arrival and my hot dusty walking clothes.

She smiled discreetly at me, said, "Oh, but certainly!" when I
asked if I could lunch there, and led me without more words to a
dark bedroom bulging with First Empire furniture, and a new
white bathroom.

When I went into the dining room it was empty of humans—a
cheerful ugly room still showing traces of the *petit bourgeois* parlor it
had been. There were aspidistras on the mantel; several small white
tables were laid with those imitation "peasant-ware" plates that one sees
in Paris china stores, and very good crystal glasses; a cat folded under
some ferns by the window ledge hardly looked at me; and the air was
softly hurried with the sound of high waters from the stream outside.

3

I waited for the maid to come back. I knew I should eat well and slowly, and suddenly the idea of dry sherry, unknown in all the village bistros of the last few days, stung my throat smoothly. I tried not to think of it; it would be impossible to realize. Dubonnet would do. But not as well. I longed for sherry.

The little maid came into the silent room. I looked at her stocky young body, and her butter-colored hair, and noticed her odd, pale voluptuous mouth before I said, "Mademoiselle, I shall drink an aperitif. Have you by any chance—"

"Let me suggest," she interrupted firmly, "our special dry sherry. It is chosen in Spain for Monsieur Paul."

And before I could agree she was gone, discreet and smooth.

She's a funny one, I thought, and waited in a pleasant warm tiredness for the wine.

It was good. I smiled approval at her, and she lowered her eyes, and then looked searchingly at me again. I realized suddenly that in this land of trained nonchalant waiters I was to be served by a small waitress who took her duties seriously. I felt much amused, and matched her solemn searching gaze.

"Today, Madame, you may eat shoulder of lamb in the English style, with baked potatoes, green beans, and a sweet."

My heart sank. I felt dismal, and hot and weary, and still grateful for the sherry.

But she was almost grinning at me, her lips curved triumphantly, and her eyes less palely blue.

"Oh, in that case," she remarked as if I had spoken, "in that case a trout, of course—a *truite au bleu* as only Monsieur Paul can prepare it!"

She glanced hurriedly at my face, and hastened on. "With the trout, one or two young potatoes—oh, very delicately boiled," she added before I could protest, "very light."

I felt better. I agreed. "Perhaps a leaf or two of salad after the fish," I suggested. She almost snapped at me. "Of course, of course! And naturally our hors d'oeuvres to commence." She started away.

"No!" I called, feeling that must assert myself now or be forever lost. "No!"

She turned back, and spoke to me very gently. "But Madame has never tasted our hors d'oeuvres. I am sure that Madame will be pleased. They are our specialty, made by Monsieur Paul himself. I am sure," and she looked reproachfully at me, her mouth tender and sad, "I am sure that Madame would be very much pleased."

I smiled weakly at her, and she left. A little cloud of hurt gentleness seemed to hang in the air where she had last stood.

I comforted myself with the sherry, feeling increasing irritation with my own feeble self. Hell! I loathed hors d'oeuvres! I conjured disgusting visions of square glass plates of oily fish, of soggy vegetables glued together with cheap mayonnaise, of rank radishes and tasteless butter. No, Monsieur Paul or not, sad young pale-faced waitress or not, I hated hors d'oeuvres.

I glanced victoriously across the room at the cat, whose eyes seemed closed.

Several minutes passed. I was really very hungry.

The door banged open, and my girl came in again, less discreet this time. She hurried toward me.

"Madame, the wine! Before Monsieur Paul can go on——" Her eyes watched my face, which I perversely kept rather glum.

"I think," I said ponderously, daring her to interrupt me, "I think that today, since I am in Burgundy and about to eat a trout," and here I hoped she noticed that I did not mention hors d'oeuvres, "I think I shall drink a bottle of Chablis 1929."

For a second her whole face blazed with joy, and then subsided into a trained mask. I knew that I had chosen well, had somehow satisfied her in a secret and incomprehensible way. She nodded politely and scuttled off, only for another second glancing impatiently at me as I called after her, "Well cooled, please, but not iced."

I'm a fool, I thought, to order a whole bottle. I'm a fool, here all alone and with more miles to walk before I reach Avallon and my fresh clothes and a bed. Then I smiled at myself and leaned back in my solid wide-seated chair, looking obliquely at the prints of Gibson girls, English tavern scenes, and hideous countrysides that hung on the papered walls. The room was warm; I could hear my companion cat purring under the ferns.

The girl rushed in, with flat baking dishes piled up her arms like the plates of a Japanese juggler. She slid them off neatly in two rows onto the table, where they lay steaming up at me, darkly and infinitely appetizing.

"*Mon Dieu!* All for me?" I peered at her. She nodded, her discretion quite gone now and a look of ecstatic worry on her pale face and eyes and lips.

There were at least eight dishes. I felt almost embarrassed, and sat for a minute looking weakly at the fork and spoon in my hand.

"Perhaps Madame would care to start with the pickled herring? It is not like any other. Monsieur Paul prepares it himself, in his own vinegar and wines. It is very good."

I dug out two or three brown filets from the dish, and tasted. They were truly unlike any others, truly the best I had ever eaten, mild, pungent, meaty as fresh nuts.

I realized the maid had stopped breathing, and looked up at her. She was watching me, or rather a gastronomic X-ray of the herring inside me, with a hypnotized glaze in her eyes.

"Madame is pleased?" she whispered softly.

I said I was. She sighed, and pushed a sizzling plate of broiled endive toward me, and disappeared.

I had put a few dull green lentils on my plate, lentils scattered with minced fresh herbs and probably marinated in tarragon vinegar and walnut oil, when she came into the dining room again with the bottle of Chablis in a wine basket.

"Madame should be eating the little baked onions while they are hot," she remarked over her shoulder as she held the bottle in a napkin and uncorked it. I obeyed meekly, and while I watched her I ate several more than I had meant to. They were delicious, simmered first in strong meat broth, I think, and then drained and broiled with olive oil and new-ground pepper.

I was fascinated by her method of uncorking a vintage wine. Instead of the Burgundian procedure of infinite and often exaggerated precautions against touching or tipping or jarring the bottle, she handled it quite nonchalantly, and seemed to be careful only to keep her hands from the cool bottle itself, holding it sometimes by the basket and sometimes in a napkin. The cork was very tight, and I thought for a minute that she would break it. So did she: her face grew tight, and did not loosen until she had slowly worked out the cork and wiped the lip. Then she poured an inch of wine in a glass, turned her

> W̲ater is for quenching thirst. Wine…is a necessary tonic, a luxury, and a fitting tribute to good food.
> —Colette, *Prisons et Paradis*

back to me like a priest taking Communion, and drank it down. Finally some was poured for me, and she stood with the bottle in her hand and her full lips drooping until I nodded a satisfied yes. Then she pushed another of the plates toward me, and almost rushed from the room.

I ate slowly, knowing that I should not be as hungry as I ought to be for the trout, but knowing too that I had never tasted such delicate savory morsels. Some were hot, some cold. The wine was light and cool. The room, warm and agreeably empty under the rushing sound of the stream, became smaller as I grew used to it.

My girl hurried in again with another row of plates up one arm, and a large bucket dragging at the other. She slid the plates deftly onto the table, and drew a deep breath as she let the bucket down against the table leg. "Your trout, Madame," she said excitedly. I looked down at the gleam of the fish curving through its limited water. "But first a good slice of Monsieur Paul's pâté. Oh yes, oh yes, you will be very sorry if you miss this. It is rich, but appetizing, and not at all too heavy. Just this one morsel!"

And willy-nilly I accepted the large gouge she dug from a terrine. I prayed for ten normal appetites and thought with amused nostalgia of my usual lunch of cold milk and fruit as I broke off a crust of bread and patted it smooth with the paste. Then I forgot everything but the exciting faint decadent flavor in my mouth.

I beamed up at the girl. She nodded, but from habit asked if I was satisfied. I beamed again, and asked, simply to please her, "Is there not a faint hint of marc, or perhaps cognac?"

"Marc, Madame!" And she awarded me the proud look of a teacher whose pupil has showed unexpected intelligence.

M arc is a spirit made from the leftovers of grapes, apples, or another fruit after pressing. It takes years for this residue to become palatable.

—LB

"Monsieur Paul, after he has taken equal parts of goose breast and the finest pork, and broken a certain number of egg yolks into them, and ground them very, very fine, cooks all with seasoning for some three hours. *But,*" she pushed her face nearer, and looked with ferocious gloating at the pâté inside me, her eyes like X-rays, "he never stops stirring it! Figure to yourself the work of it—stir, stir, never stopping!

"Then he grinds in a suspicion of nutmeg, and then adds, very thoroughly, a glass of marc for each hundred grams of pâté. And is Madame not pleased?"

Again I agreed, rather timidly, that Madame was much pleased, that Madame had never, indeed, tasted such an unctuous and exciting pâté. The girl wet her lips delicately, and then started as if she had been pin-stuck.

"But the trout! My God, the trout!" She grabbed the bucket, and her voice grew higher and more rushed.

"Here is the trout, Madame. You are to eat it *au bleu,* and you should never do so if you had not seen it alive. For if the trout were dead when it was plunged into the court bouillon it would not turn blue. So, naturally, it must be living."

I knew all this, more or less, but I was fascinated by her absorption in the momentary problem. I felt quite ignorant, and asked her with sincerity, "What about the trout? Do you take out its guts before or after?"

"Oh, the trout!" She sounded scornful. "Any trout is glad, truly glad, to be prepared by Monsieur Paul. His little gills are pinched, with one flash of the knife he is empty, and then he curls in agony in the bouillon and all is over. And it is the curl you must judge, Madame. A false *truite au bleu* cannot curl."

She panted triumph at me, and hurried out with the bucket.

She *is* a funny one, I thought, and for not more than two or three minutes I drank wine and mused over her. Then she darted in, with the trout correctly blue and agonizingly curled on a platter, and on her crooked arm a plate of tiny boiled potatoes and a bowl.

When I had been served and had cut off her anxious breathings with an assurance that the fish was the best I had ever tasted, she peered again at me and at the sauce in the bowl. I obediently put some of it on the potatoes: no fool I, to ruin *truite au bleu* with a hot concoction! There was more silence.

"Ah!" she sighed at last. "I knew Madame would feel thus! Is it not the most beautiful sauce in the world with the flesh of a trout?"

I nodded incredulous agreement.

"Would you like to know how it is done?"

I remembered all the legends of chefs who guarded favorite recipes with their very lives, and murmured yes.

She wore the exalted look of a believer describing a miracle at Lourdes as she told me, in a rush, how Monsieur Paul threw chopped chives into hot sweet butter and then poured the butter off, how he added another nut of butter and a tablespoonful of thick cream for each person, stirred the mixture for a few minutes over a slow fire, and then rushed it to the table.

"So simple?" I asked softly, watching her lighted eyes and the tender lustful lines of her strange mouth.

"So simple, Madame! But," she shrugged, "you know, with a master—"

I was relieved to see her go: such avid interest in my eating wore on me. I felt released when the door closed behind her, free for a minute or so from her victimization. What would she have done, I wondered, if I had been ignorant or unconscious of any fine flavors?

She was right, though, about Monsieur Paul. Only a master could live in this isolated mill and preserve his gastronomic dignity through loneliness and the sure financial loss of unused butter and addled eggs. Of course there was the stream for his fish, and I knew his pâtés would grow even more edible with age; but how could he manage to have a thing like roasted lamb ready for any chance patron? Was the consuming interest of his one maid enough fuel for his flame?

I tasted the last sweet nugget of trout, the one nearest the blued tail, and poked somnolently at the minute white billiard balls that had been eyes. Fate could not harm me, I remembered winily, for I had indeed dined today, and dined well. Now for a leaf of crisp salad, and I'd be on my way.

The girl slid into the room. She asked me again, in a respectful but gossipy manner, how I had liked this and that and the other things, and then talked on as she mixed dressing for the endive.

"And now," she announced, after I had eaten one green sprig and dutifully pronounced it excellent, "now Madame is going to taste Monsieur Paul's special terrine, one that is not even on the summer menu, when a hundred covers are laid here daily and we have a headwaiter and a wine waiter, and cabinet ministers telegraph for tables! Madame will be pleased."

And heedless of my low moans of the walk still before me, of my appreciation and my unhappily human and limited capacity, she cut a thick heady slice from the terrine of meat and stood over me while I ate it, telling me with almost hysterical pleasure of the wild ducks, the spices, the wines that went into it. Even surfeit could not make me deny that it was a rare dish. I ate it all, knowing my luck, and wishing only that I had red wine to drink with it.

I was beginning, though, to feel almost frightened, realizing myself an accidental victim of these stranded gourmets, Monsieur Paul and his handmaiden. I began to feel that they were using me for a safety valve, much as a thwarted women relieves herself with tantrums or a fit of weeping. I was serving a purpose, and perhaps a noble one, but I resented it in a way approaching panic.

I protested only to myself when one of Monsieur Paul's special cheeses was cut for me, and ate it doggedly, like a slave. When the girl said that Monsieur Paul himself was preparing a special filter of coffee for me, I smiled servile acceptance: wine and the weight of the food and my own character could not force me to argue with maniacs. When, before the coffee came, Monsieur Paul presented me, through his idolater, with the most beautiful apple tart I had ever seen, I allowed it to be cut and served to me. Not a wince or a murmur showed the waitress my distressed fearfulness. With a stuffed careful smile on my face, and a clear nightmare in my head of trussed wanderers prepared for his altar by this hermit-priest of gastronomy, I listened to the girl's passionate plea for fresh pastry dough.

"You cannot, you *cannot*, Madame, serve old pastry!" She seemed ready to beat her breast as she leaned across the table. "Look at that delicate crust! You may feel that you have eaten too much." (I nodded idiotic agreement.) "But this pastry is like feathers—it is like snow. It is in fact good for you, a digestive! And why?" She glared sternly at me. "Because Monsieur Paul did not even open the flour bin until he saw you coming! He could not, he *could* not have baked you one of his special apple tarts with old dough!"

Cycling past a local *boulangerie*, I caught a whiff of that inescapably delicious aroma of fresh-baking bread, so I quickly decided that a stop in the bakery would easily compensate for whatever notes I might miss by being late for class. I pointed to the first roll-like item I saw in the glass case, paid the four-franc price, and leapt back on my bike. I mark my true discovery of self from that moment. As I bit into the delectable crust and found the stick of slightly melted, utterly *chocolate* chocolate baked inside the pastry, I knew I had found my true culinary passion. For me, travel in France has never been the same.

—Mary V. Davidson,
"The Pain of Chocolate"

She laughed, tossing back her head and curling her mouth voluptuously.

Somehow I managed to refuse a second slice, but I trembled under her surmise that I was ready for my special filter.

The wine and its fortitude had fled me, and I drank the hot coffee as a suffering man gulps ether, deeply and gratefully.

I remember, then, chatting with surprising glibness, and sending Monsieur Paul flowery compliments, all of them sincere and well won, and I remember feeling only amusement when a vast glass of marc appeared before me and then gradually disappeared, like the light in the warm room full of water-sounds. I felt surprise to be alive still, and suddenly very grateful to the wild-lipped waitress, as if her presence had sustained me through duress. We discussed food and wine. I wondered bemusedly why I had been frightened.

The marc was gone. I went into the crowded bedroom for my jacket. She met me in the darkening hall when I came out, and I paid my bill, a large one. I started to thank her, but she took my hand, drew me into the dining room, and without words poured more spirits into my glass. I drank to Monsieur Paul while she watched me intently, her pale eyes bulging in the dimness and her lips pressed inward as she too tasted the hot, aged marc.

The cat rose from his ferny bed, and walked contemptuously out of the room.

Suddenly the girl began to laugh, in a soft shy breathless way, and came close to me.

"Permit me!" she said, and I thought she was going to kiss me. But instead she pinned a tiny bunch of snowdrops and dark bruised cyclamens against my stiff jacket, very quickly and deftly, and then ran from the room with her head down.

I waited for a minute. No sounds came from anywhere in the old mill, but the endless rushing of the full stream seemed to strengthen, like the timed blare of an orchestra under a falling curtain.

She's a *funny* one, I thought. I touched the cool blossoms on my coat and went out, like a ghost from ruins, across the courtyard toward the dim road to Avallon.

Mary Francis Kennedy (M.F.K.) Fisher was widely regarded in the middle of the twentieth century as the finest writer of prose in America. She said that her chief responsibility as a writer was "to write the good and pleasing sentence." Of her many works, some of her better known are: How to Cook a

Wolf; Consider the Oyster; The Gastronomical Me; An Alphabet for Gourmets; *and* Serve Forth. *This story is found in her book,* As They Were. *She died in 1992.*

Waiting for *Gözleme*

In a race against time, hunger is everything.

We'd been exploring the wonders of Cappadocia in Central Turkey, marveling at the man-made and geological beauty of the area. Bright, colorful frescoes adorned the walls of churches, the oldest carved from the rocks more than 1,300 years ago. Beautiful rock formations known as fairy chimneys filled valleys with their strange forms. From the soft porous rock of the area emerged Zelve, a whole village of troglodyte dwellings that had been inhabited until quite recently.

Throughout the long day, my friend and I had forgotten about eating, distracted by the sights around us. Finally, as we headed to the bus stop in Zelve to catch the last bus back to Ürgüp, due in at six o'clock, we remembered that we hadn't eaten since breakfast. A typical Turkish breakfast offered massive amounts of food—bread, cheese, olives, tomatoes, cucumbers, hard-boiled eggs—and was usually enough to tide us over. But not today. When the hunger pangs hit we immediately started to talk about what we'd eat for dinner once we arrived.

We got to the bus stop with little time to spare, and that's when we saw two women sitting on the side of the road, a mother and daughter team, selling fresh *gözleme*. Both were beautiful, with long

14

dark hair, loosely covered with a simple beaded headscarf. They were wearing the traditional dress of the area—a gauzy peasant blouse on top and baggy colorful pants on the bottom. They smiled at us and pointed to a large griddle by their side, offering to cook us some *gözleme*. I'd never tasted *gözleme*, a mixture of cheeses and spices wrapped in fresh dough and cooked over a hot griddle, but Kenan had, and he said that we should try it. I looked at my watch; I looked at the women and the griddle, a bowl of dough sitting next to it. I told Kenan that we didn't have time, but in the spirit of adventure, he said, "Let's try. We'll pay the women anyway if it's not ready when the bus comes."

Kenan explained to the mother that we had to catch the six o'clock bus back to Ürgüp, and immediately I saw something sparkle in her eyes when she met his gaze. I saw that she was determined to take on the challenge, to work against the clock. She looked back at him, intensely, gravely, seriously—the way that Turks can often look—and told him, "You will have your *gözleme*." Then she stood up and ordered her daughter to a shack a hundred or so feet away, and the daughter went off like a gazelle.

The mother turned up the heat on the griddle and took out two clumps of dough from the bowl. She began to roll out the dough, an expert at the task, this way and that, back and forth, a miracle before my eyes: in seconds, the thinnest, most perfectly round pieces of dough I'd ever seen. Just as she finished rolling, the daughter returned, panting, with a bowl of the filling—fresh cheese, parsley, red pepper, other spices, salt and pepper. The mother quickly flipped the dough onto the griddle, turned it once, sprinkled the filling over the dough, and I saw it beginning to happen: the birth of my first *gözleme*.

And then we heard it, all of us, in the distance, the *dolmuş*—a minibus whose name means stuffed—on its way to Zelve. We all looked up to see it, rattling over the narrow road, working its way down to where we stood, suspended in the moment. It still had a few curves to take, a hill or two to climb and descend before it would arrive. But we all knew in an instant that we wouldn't make it; that it was a good try, but it wouldn't work; that the filling in the *gözleme* wouldn't melt just right; and the raw dough over the filling wouldn't cook just right in the amount of time that we had left before the bus arrived in Zelve.

As the bus approached, we tried to stop the women, tried to give them money anyway, tried to thank them for a valiant effort. But they wouldn't hear of it, and they insisted on continuing, the *gözleme* beginning to sizzle on the griddle. When the bus driver opened the door, Kenan and I stood still for a moment, not sure what to do. But the mother, she knew. *Maybe she has done this before*, I thought. She jumped up and asked the bus driver to wait for a moment.

He resisted.

She begged.

He resisted some more.

She implored. *"Lütfen, lütfen."* Please, please, she nearly wailed. Wouldn't he please, *lütfen*, hold on, rest a moment, wait until the *gözleme* was finished. It wouldn't be a huge problem now, would it? "And look," she pointed to us, "the visitors are starving."

We put on sad faces and tried to look really hungry, while I added in the best Turkish I could, *"Çok aç"* (very hungry) as the bus driver roared and moaned, protested profusely, claimed that he couldn't wait at every bus stop on his route for meals to be made. But she argued her case well, and she argued it long, and all the time she argued, the *gözleme* sizzled and sizzled, and the aroma from the griddle rose up from the side of the road, wafted through the open doors of the bus, and made its way slowly and purposefully down the aisle. Suddenly, I heard a sympathetic voice rise up from the back of the bus: "Oh come on, I don't mind waiting a little bit. Let them have their *gözleme*." And soon another voice joined that voice. Until eventually we had the support of everyone on the bus to wait out the cooking of the *gözleme*. "What's the big rush anyway?" someone from a front seat asked.

The bus driver turned to face the mutinous crowd of passengers behind him, and finally shrugged his shoulders, turned back to the mother, and said, "Okay. Okay. *Tamam*. But don't ask this of me again."

And so the bus waited at the Zelve bus stop while the women finished cooking our *gözleme*. The mother folded the dough over the filling as if she were sealing an envelope with a secret message inside. When it was all done, the dough was perfectly cooked, light brown spots dotting the outside, the cheese soft and warm, the spices just beginning to send out their flavor. The daughter wrapped up one and the mother wrapped up another as we paid for the food and then jumped onto the bus. Someone on the bus cheered as we sat down, and a few other passengers joined him. I smiled at everyone on the bus, a little embarrassed, but happy too to have my *gözleme*. We turned and waved to the women on the side of the road, now settling back down, squatting next to their hot griddle.

We sat on the bus, and the sun sank further into the Cappadocia landscape as we ate our *gözleme*, one of the best, and certainly one of the hardest won meals I had in Turkey.

Pier Roberts lives and works in Los Angeles, California. Her stories have appeared in Travelers' Tales Spain, A Woman's Passion for Travel, Escape, *and* Atlantic Unbound.

ASHLEY PALMER

At War with Grandma

Where food is a weapon and defeat is delicious.

GRANDMOTHERS AND FOOD. FOR BETTER OR FOR WORSE, THERE is an undeniable connection between the two. Your grandmother may have tempted you with homemade apple pie that magically appeared from her oven as you walked in the door. Or perhaps you dreaded grandma's mystery casserole, developed from a recipe she dug up from the Dark Ages. You may have had a grandma who lovingly indulged you with the sweets forbidden by your own parents. Or maybe she was the one who most despaired of your picky eating habits by nagging, "Your mother loved this when she was your age, why won't *you* eat it?" While living in Japan, I found that this connection between grandmothers and food not only exists cross-culturally, but also, in my case, extended to include a surrogate Japanese grandmother.

I was introduced to Kobayashi-san by my university advisor, who lived in the same village. When we met, I was approaching the end of a year living in Nagano Prefecture, researching Japanese rural lifestyles. My advisor had arranged for me to work with Kobayashi-san several days a week, helping out at her home, where she cultivated and sold bonsai and other plants.

It wasn't only the connection with food that made Kobayashi-san seem grandmotherly. Neither was it merely her age. At seventy-five, she puttered around her gardens from dawn to dusk, her bent frame moving up and down the rows of plants, muttering to herself constantly. She immediately gave up on the difficult pronunciation of my name, and adopted the more familiar nickname, "Ah-chan." She also didn't hesitate to put me to work, weeding, stacking news-papers, washing dishes. But what most made her a grandmother in my mind was that telltale combination of being simultaneously con-cerned, critical, frank, and affectionate. One minute she would scold me for refusing to wear a hat in the sun, and the next minute she would insist I was working too hard. Unlike many Japanese, who initially hide behind a wall of social formality, Kobayashi-san was surprisingly forward with me, and seemed unphased by our cultural and linguistic differences. Being so far from home and my own two wonderful grandmothers, I found her acceptance of me endearing.

It all started rather innocently. There was a steady stream of people flowing in and out of her home. Some were customers, but most were local people, looking for conversation, gossip, or just a friendly face. Keeping with the custom in Japan, she religiously served tea and snacks to all the visitors who joined her at the big table. It was there, on my first day, that she asked me, "Do you like Japanese food?" I replied promptly in the affirmative. It could have been that I answered too confidently, or she may have just wanted to have a little fun. But, looking back to that day, I swear there was a gleam in her eye when she responded, "Oh really?"

I do love Japanese food. Moreover, I felt that during the previous ten months I had developed an appreciation for the cuisine that had been lacking during my prior experiences living in Japan. Raw fish so fresh and soft it melts in your mouth. The simplicity of cold soba noodles slurped on a summer afternoon. However, I had never claimed to love every type of Japanese food. I knew of the differ-ences between mainstream Japanese cuisine and local country spe-cialties, having once been offered candied grasshoppers on a research trip to the same village. But this time it wasn't the food itself that took me by surprise, but rather the spirit in which Kobayashi-san offered it.

Kobayashi-san prided herself on having a variety of snacks to offer her guests, and on that first day she deliberately arranged several bowls of cookies, crackers, and pickles around my place. As I reached for a mild-looking rice cracker, she intercepted my hand mid-reach and pushed something else into it. "I bet you've never tried this before. I don't know if you'll like it, but you should try it!" she challenged. I cast a longing glance in the direction of my rice cracker and opened my hand to reveal a much more menacing seafood snack. It was a dried fish, the chewy kind meant to be consumed whole—bones, tail, and head. I gnawed on it tentatively and, finding the taste bearable, I politely responded, "It's good, really!" Kobayashi-san threw back her head and laughed, her eyes crinkling up until they almost disappeared into the wrinkles on her face.

> The sushi chef handed us a beautiful plate of raw fish. The sashimi was laid out in strips and adorned with colorful greenery. Behind that, a disfigured fish was elegantly displayed on a skewer. Its head, backbone, and tail were still intact; the only parts missing were its fleshy sides. As we looked down at our dinner, the fish's mouth began to open and close, gasping for its last breaths. All of a sudden we didn't feel so hungry anymore.
> —Laura Peterson, "Sashimi Anyone?"

The next time I visited Kobayashi-san, she disappeared into the kitchen upon my arrival, leaving me to wonder what was in store. When she emerged, she was holding an ancient, battered saucepan that proclaimed, "Bear Orchestra: We are bear orchestra. We love music very much." The contents looked harmless, like warm milk, but when she poured two generous servings, little lumps kerplopped from the pan into the teacups. She announced cheerfully, "We make this out of rice and sake. You probably won't like it, but maybe you want to try it!" I took a sip. Like the fish snack, it wasn't bad. But by the time I had choked half of it down, the starchy, lumpy, alcohol flavor had become too much for me and I put my cup down in defeat. She again laughed heartily and chided me, saying, "I didn't think you would like it much!"

That was also the day Kobayashi-san decided, in a very grand-motherly way, that I couldn't possibly be trusted to prepare an acceptable bag lunch on my own, so she would feed me lunch on the days I came to visit. Therefore, I would be completely at her mercy, a helpless target for any weird food she could dream up.

As I pulled weeds that morning, I gave some thought to the odd situation in which I found myself. This sweet, kind old lady was so determined to challenge the limits of my palate, and was making no effort whatsoever to disguise her intention to get the best of me. However, I detected nothing malicious or underhanded in her challenge. Her laughter made it abundantly clear that it was all in good fun. With this in mind, I decided to take her on as a worthy adversary. Frankly, after ten months in Japan, I was beginning to stagger under the weight of Japanese social formality, endless small talk, and unnecessary politeness. I embraced the chance to found a friendship on plain old fun. I admit that I was motivated, in part, by pride. I wanted very much to show that Americans could eat more than just the greasy, fatty, rich foods with which we are often asso-ciated. So I harnessed my fighting spirit in the field that day, and prepared to mount a formidable defense from that point on.

Because our little competition remained largely unspoken, I made up my own rules. In order to claim victory, I had to finish the whole portion of what I was given. I also had to keep a straight face. A grimace from me would be a victory for her. I had won the bat-tle with the dried fish snack, but she had emerged victorious with the rice drink, so we would officially begin with a victory apiece.

Like most wars, even those fought in jest, we each won some battles and lost some battles. Over the next four weeks, I was served all kinds of strange and unappetizing Japanese food. Every imagin-able type of salted and dried seafood. Pickles so strong I had to gaze out at the mountains and inhale deeply to avoid grimacing. A vari-ety of mysterious "mountain vegetables," (essentially any edible plant plucked from the surrounding hills) heaped with fish flakes. Kobayashi-san was tricky, and sometimes she changed her tactics.

She didn't always focus on taste, but came at me with texture, as well. When I accidentally let it slip that I had no particular problem eating squid, she soon produced some sort of snack consisting of whole squid, glistening in an unnatural, clear gel. They were so slippery and slimy I could barely manage to get ahold of one with my chopsticks, and the texture played tricks with my senses, making it seem as though the squid was alive in my mouth. I accepted defeat gratefully on that day.

Another memorable battle was fought over a seemingly innocent grilled fish. Anyone who has lived in Japan knows that the Japanese are trained practically from birth to eat fish efficiently, separating the bones from the flesh with little waste. The trick is to avoid disturbing the fish's skeletal form as you eat. I was aware of the need to extract the flesh with caution, but despite my respectable chopstick skills, I managed to mangle the skeleton within seconds, and was left ungracefully pulling bones from my mouth with each bite. The fish she had served was the boniest I had ever seen, yet she grinned at me over her own orderly pile of bones, picked clean with enviable precision.

As my time working with Kobayashi-san neared its end, I realized we were approaching the finish line essentially neck and neck. I felt that our little game shouldn't end without a winner, so I decided to set the stage for a final battle. I would turn the tables and bring a little treat for Kobayashi-san, a homemade goody to offer in appreciation of her hospitality.

Was I out of line to even consider mounting an offensive? Do good girls retaliate against their grandmother's questionable cooking? I felt a brief stab of guilt as I considered these issues, but in the end my competitive side overcame my polite and cautious side. However, I wouldn't let it get out of hand. I would follow the guidelines she had established, and make something that I thought would genuinely challenge her, but something authentically American, and something I personally found delicious. I decided to make brownies.

Many Japanese, particularly older Japanese, don't care for the super-sweet, rich desserts in which so many of us Westerners overindulge. Japanese cakes and cookies are tame in comparison to their American cousins. The lavishly decorated cakes in a Japanese bakery can be deceiving. One bite reveals all too often that they are quite bland by our standards. American desserts are decadent, Japanese desserts are dainty. The Japanese pick at their pie with miniature dessert forks, while we Americans scoop our hot fudge sundaes with shovels. All things considered, brownies were a pretty good bet to represent Team America in this international food challenge.

In keeping with the spirit of the game, I used an authentic American recipe to make a deliciously rich and sweet pan of brownies. Two whole sticks of butter, a cup and a half of sugar, two hefty pieces of chocolate. In order to placate my slightly guilty conscience, I resisted the urge to deviate from the original recipe by adding chocolate chips. When I took the pan out of the oven, I was so overcome by the enticing aroma that I had no choice but to immediately gobble down two brownies, licking my buttery fingers to savor the last morsel. They were lovely, and every bit as choco-latey, dense, and rich as I had hoped.

The next morning, before I had the chance to eat the rest of the pan myself, I wrapped six brownies in tin foil and headed off to Kobayashi-san's house. As I put them on the big table I said, "These are probably too sweet, but please have one. It's an American treat I made for you." I noted the somewhat surprised smile on her face as she leaned in to take one. A hundred thoughts crossed my mind in the time it took to raise that brownie to her lips. She'll hate it. She'll spit it out. She'll take a couple of polite bites and then say it's too early in the day for sweets. But the next thing I heard was, "This is really good!" I knew that would be her response regardless of her true opinion, so I watched her face as she ate it. I watched her take one bite, then another bite, and another, until the whole brownie was gone.

Well, that was it. She had finished her portion with a smile on her face and earned herself the victory. Not just the battle, but the whole war. Team America had been crushed and would accept defeat. Looking into Kobayashi-san's eyes at that moment, I wondered if she knew. I wondered if she knew my full intention in offering her the brownies. I wondered if she had guessed that I was half-hoping she would hate my food. I wondered if she knew about the rules of the game I had made up, and that I had conceded defeat. And then, as I held the gaze of my Japanese grandmother, she smiled, and reached for another brownie…and devoured it before my eyes.

Ashley Palmer recently returned from one year of studying in Japan with the help of the Japan-United States Education Commission and a Fulbright research scholarship. She returned home to Massachusetts to consume large quantities of decadent desserts and search for new ways to return to Asia.

Sfuso: Loose Wine

*A day in the Tuscan countryside
comes home in a bottle.*

GITA, ONE OF MY FAVORITE WORDS, A LITTLE TRIP. THIS MORNING, I expected my husband Ed to head to the olive terraces with his hoe but instead, he looked up from Burton Anderson's *The Wine Atlas of Italy*, which he often reads at breakfast, and said, "Let's go to Montepulciano. Our wine supply is getting low."

"Great. I want to go to the garden center there to buy plumbago to plant under the hazelnut tree. And we can pick up fresh ricotta at a farm."

Isn't this what we came to Italy for? Sometimes, in the long restoration, I've thought that I came to Italy only to rip ivy from walls and refinish floors. But now that the main projects are over, the house is—well, not finished, but at least looking more like home.

We will restock our *sfuso*, loose wine. Many vineyards produce a house wine for themselves, their friends, and local customers. Most Tuscans don't drink bottled wine on an everyday basis; either they make their own, they know someone who does, or they buy *sfuso*. In preparation, Ed washes out our enormous green glass demijohn and also our shiny, stainless steel container with a red spigot, an innovation that threatens to replace the traditional demijohns.

To protect wine from air after the demijohn is filled, we learned to pour a splash of olive oil on top, forming a seal, then jam in a fist-sized cork. The new canister has a flat lid which floats on top of the wine. A drizzle of neutral oil is poured around the tiny space between the lid and the side of the canister. A second tight lid then goes on top. As you open the spigot at the bottom and pour your wine into a pitcher, the lid and sealing oil lower too, keeping the seal intact.

When families have seven or eight demijohns, they usually store them in a special cool room, a cantina, then uncork each demijohn as they need wine. We've done that, hoisted the demijohn to a table and tipped it, filling old wine bottles through a funnel, then sealed our twenty or so bottles with olive oil. We became adept at tossing off the oil with a jerk when we opened the bottle. But always a few drops floated on the surface. Already, I've consigned two demijohns to decorative functions in corners of rooms. We found our three abandoned by the recycle bin; someone else had given up. But how could they throw the bottles away? I love the curvaceous, globular, pregnant shape and the green glass with bubbles trapped inside. We scrubbed them with bottle brushes made for the job and bought new corks. "Do we really want to use the demijohn again?" I venture.

"You're right. But don't tell the men." He means, of course, Anselmo, Beppe, and Francesco, who scorn any change regarding olives or wine. We load two twenty-liter plastic jugs into the truck—handy for transporting, but we must transfer the wine into the canister as soon as we come home. A plastic taste can seep quickly into wine.

It's great being a tourist. Guidebook and camera in my bag, a bottle of water in the car, the map spread out on my knees—what could be finer?

The road from Cortona to Montepulciano, one of my favorites, levels from terraced olive groves to luxive, undulating hills, brilliant with golden wheels of wheat in summer, and now in spring, bright green with cover crops and long grasses. I can almost see the July fields in bloom with *girasoli*, giant sunflowers, the hallelujah chorus of crops. Today, lambs are out. The new ones look whiffey on their faltering legs, while those just older cavort about the mothers' udders. This is the sweetest countryside I know. Only occasional blasts of pig barn odors remind me that this is not paradise. In shadowed dips of the hills, shaggy flocks sleep in big white clumps. Wheat fields, fruit orchards, and olives, perfectly cared for inch by inch—all gradually give way to the vineyards of Vino Nobile of Montepulciano.

Chianti, Brunello, and Vino Nobile, the three greatest wines of Tuscany, share a characteristic full-bodied, essential grape taste. Beyond that, Tuscans can discuss endless shades of difference far into the night. Since production of Vino Nobile began in the 1300s, they've had a long time to get it just right. The name of the Tuscan grape, Sangiovese, suggests much older wine production; the etymology is from *sanguis*, Latin for "blood," and from Jove—blood of Jove. The local strain of Sangiovese is called *"prugnolo gentile,"* nice little plums.

Sangiovese is grown extensively in central Italy and is used to form the basis for Chianti, Torgiano, Montefalco, and other wines. It is redolent with sweet cherry and leather tones which, when aged, are lovely but when made poorly can be harsh and unpleasant. Sangiovese is a fine match with a variety of recipes, including pasta and pizza.

—LB

We turn into a long alley of lofty cypresses lining a *strada bianca*, a white road tunneling under the trees. We drive through gaps between trees. Ed only nods when I remember a line from Octavio Paz, "Light is time thinking about itself." It seems true to me on one level and not on another. The Avignonesi vineyards surround one of those sublime properties that set me to dreaming of living in another life in an earlier time. The villa, the family chapel, the noble outbuildings—I'm in a heavy linen dress in 1780, sweeping across the courtyard, a white pitcher and a ring of iron keys in my hands. Whether I'm the *contessa* of this *fattoria* or the maid, I don't know, but I have a flash of my steps years ago, the outline of my shadow on the stones.

Avignonesi's winemaker, Paolo Trappolini, a startlingly good-looking man who looks like a Raphael portrait of himself, tells us about the experiments at the vineyard. "I've been searching out almost-extinct rootstock around Tuscany and saving old strains." We walk out in the vineyard and he shows us new bushy vines planted in the *settonce* pattern, a Latin way of placing one vine in the center of a hexagon of other plants. He points uphill at a spiraling planting pattern, *la vigna tonda,* the round vineyard. "This also is an experiment in using different densities to see the effect on wine quantity and quality." He shows us the aging rooms, some of which are covered in thick, gray mold, and the *vin santo* room, deliriously perfumed with smoky, woody scents.

Avignonesi makes many fine wines which can be tasted here or in their Palazzo Avignonesi in the center of Montepulciano. Ed is especially interested in their *vin santo,* the smooth, nutty wine sipped with biscotti after dinner. In homes, at all hours, we've been offered *vin santo,* have had *vin santo* forced on us. It's ready, in every cupboard, and you must try it because it's homemade. Avignonesi's is special, one of Italy's finest. We are able to buy only one bottle; their limited quantity has been sold. Someone has given us two venerable bottles of *vin santo,* a 1953 and a 1962 Ricasoli, bought in New York and now transported back to their place of origin. Anselmo also has given us a bottle of his own. With the precious Avignonesi, we'll invite friends for a tasting after a big feast one summer night.

Next is Tenuta Trerose. Most of their vineyards are planted the usual way, in staked rows, but a large field is planted as a low arbor, the Etruscan style of planting. The offices are in a modern building behind a villa in a cypress grove. A young man, surprised to see visitors, gives us a price list and shows us their wines in a conference room. Ed, having consulted the most recent *Vini d'Italia,* his trusty yearly guide, selects a case of Salterio Chardonnay and a mixed case of reds. We follow the man out onto a catwalk overlooking a warehouse of stainless steel tanks, some oak barrels, and cases and cases of wine. He shouts, and a woman appears from behind boxes. She starts to put together our cases, leaping, as gracefully as a lynx, over and on stacks of boxes.

Inconspicuous yellow signs point the way to vineyards—Fassato, Massimo Romeo, Villa S. Anna (produced by women), Fattoria del Cerro, Terre di Bindella, Podere Il Macchione, Valdipiatta. We know the names, having popped many a cork from their heroic wines. We're headed to Poliziano for our *sfuso*. Ed waves to someone in a field, who meets us in their warehouse. "The best *sfuso* in a decade," he tells us, as he sets out two glasses on a stack of wine boxes. Even at 11 A.M., we're pleased by the hearty red color and the light hint of strawberries in the taste and, what, oh, almost a fragrance of mimosa. We've found our house wine. He fills our jugs from a hose attached to an enormous vat. By law he must seal the jugs and dutifully record our names in his computer. As he pulls up Ed's name, he sees we've been here before. "Americans like our wine, no?" he asks, so we answer yes, for all Americans. Ed wedges the tanks behind the seat, hoping they won't leak as we negotiate unpaved roads.

The sanguine town of Montepulciano stretches and winds as though it were following a river but it climbs a long ridge instead. Henry James's impression, a view caught between arcades, was of "some big battered, blistered, overladen, overmasted ship, swimming in a violet sea." Tuscan hilltowns often give one the sense of an immense ship sailing above a plain.

On the roof across from Sant'Agostino, an iron *pulcinella* has hit the clock with his hammer to mark all the hours since the 1600s. I stop to buy candles in a small shop. There, among the potholders, key rings, mats, and corkscrews, I find a dim opening into an Etruscan tomb! "Oh yes," the owner says as he flicks on spotlights, "many store owners find these surprises when they renovate." He leads us over to a glass-covered opening in the front of the shop and points. We look down into a deep cistern hollowed from stone. He shrugs. "The roof drained here so they always had water."

"When?" Ed asks.

The owner lights a cigarette and blows smoke against the window. "The Middle Ages, possibly earlier." We're always amazed by how casually Italians accept their coexistence with such remains of the past.

The street up to the *centro storico*, historic center, jogs off the main shopping street so that the piazza is somewhat removed from the bustle of daily shopping. The unfinished front of the massive church adds to the abandoned feeling. A sheepdog on the steps is the most alert being in the piazza. We don't go in this time, but, walking by, I imagine inside the polyptych altarpiece by Taddeo di Bartolo, where Mary is dying in one panel, then surrounded by lovely angels while being swooped into heaven, with apostles weeping down on earth. White plastic café chairs lean onto their tables in one corner of the piazza. We have the whole grand, majestic square to ourselves. We look down into the bottomless well, presided over by two stone lions and two griffins. It must have been a pleasure to shoulder your jug and go to the town well to meet your friends and haul up pure water.

In the fine palazzi, several vineyards have tasting rooms. Inside Poliziano's, there's a portrait of the Renaissance poet for whom this distinguished vineyard is named. The woman who pours liberal tastes highly recommends two of their reserve wines and she is right. Three of their wines are named for poems of Poliziano's: Le Stanze, Ambrae, and Elegia. Stanzas and Elegy we understand but what does the white wine's name, *ambrae*, mean? She pauses then shakes her head. Finally she waves her hands, smiles, *"Solo ambrae, ambrae."* She gestures everywhere. Ambiance is my best guess. We buy several reserve and the poet's wines.

As a poet, Poliziano made it big in Montepulciano. A bar on the main street is named for him, too, though the décor is strictly nineteenth century instead of the poet's period. Beyond the curved marble bar are two rooms of dark wood and William Morris–style wallpaper with matching upholstered banquettes and proper little round tables, a Victorian tearoom, Italian style. Both rooms open onto the view, framed by flower-filled iron balconies. We have a sandwich and coffee then hurry to the car. The day is slipping away. I stop for a quick look at a church interior I remember, the Chiesa del Gesù, with its small *trompe l'oeil* dome painted to look like an encircling stair rail around another dome. The perspective only makes sense to the eye from the center of the front entrance. From any other, it goes wonky.

The flower nursery takes its name from the massive church, San Biagio, which we skirt quickly in our rush to buy the plumbago before closing. San Biagio is one of my favorite buildings in the world, for its position at the end of a cypress-lined drive, and for its golden stones, which radiate in afternoon sun, casting a soft flush on the faces of those looking up at the austere planes of the building. If you sit on one of the ledges around the base, the light pours over you, while also seeming to seep into your back from the walls. A walk around the building, inside the warm halo surrounding it, gives me a sense of well-being. As we wind around San Biagio on the road going down, we see the church from changing angles.

We find an apricot bougainvillea to replace one that froze, two plumbagos promising soft blue clusters of bloom under the trees, and a new rose, Pierre de Ronsard, a climber for a stone wall. A French poet to join Poliziano in the car.

One evening toward week's end, we give ourselves a break and hire a chef for the evening. Fanni doesn't speak a word of English but she proclaims the understated pleasures of Umbrian cuisine in her cooking. We dine al fresco under a grape arbor. Paula concedes it might be the setting that makes this night a unanimous favorite. "Each course is accompanied by a different sky, a new backdrop for each dish," she notices. A golden sunset for the crostini appetizers; blazing pink peaks for the first plate of lasagna; a dramatic azure horizon fades into darkness as we're served the roasted chicken. There's nothing left to do other than applaud Fanni's efforts. I think, too, we are applauding the abundance of this country retreat. And ourselves for taking none of it for granted.

—Iyna Bort Caruso,
"When a Cucina Says Yes"

"Oh, no." Ed hits his fist on the steering wheel.

"What?"

"We forgot to stop for ricotta." The ricotta farms are near Pienza, miles down the road.

The mingled scents of plants and sloshing wine wash through the car, along with the deep grassy smell of spring rain which has begun to fall as we head toward Cortona.

For dinner tonight, we've stopped at the *rosticceria* and picked up some divine gnocchi made from semolina flour. I've made a salad. Ed brings out the Ambrae from Montepulciano and holds it up to the light. Ambrae is not in my dictionary. It must be Latin, possibly for amber. I take a sip—maybe it is ambiance, the way dew on lilacs and oak leaves might taste. Wine is light, held together by water. I wish I'd said that, but Galileo did.

Frances Mayes has written for The New York Times, House Beautiful, *and* Food and Wine. *Her books include* Under the Tuscan Sun: At Home in Italy *and* Bella Tuscany: The Sweet Life in Italy, *from which this story was excerpted. She divides her time between Cortona, Italy and San Francisco, California.*

FAITH ADIELE

Tempted in Jakarta

What would happen if she stopped just once?

I COME UPON THE JAKARTA PIZZA HUT FEELING A BIT EXTRAVAGANT
and giddy. I have spent days trudging around fetid, steaming Jakarta,
my least favorite Asian city, black tears of pollution streaming down
my sticky cheeks, getting the bureaucratic run-around. I am tired of
being in transit, tired of worrying about potential thieves and fakirs,
tired of trying to squeeze myself into native life. At last my stolen
traveler's checks have been replaced, and in two hours I have a flight
out of this labyrinth of rubbish heaps and open sewers.

I stand outside the Jakarta Pizza Hut, bastion of Western culture,
feeling at once compelled and repelled. It looks like any Pizza Hut
anywhere in the USA, and I haven't eaten for thirty hours. Still I
hesitate. I pride myself on being a true traveler, able to withstand
hardship, scornful of Western luxury. As I ponder, it begins to
rain—big black drops that sizzle ominously as they hit the street.

The inside of the Jakarta Pizza Hut is nearly empty. A young
waiter ushers me to a table with all the pomp and ceremony due a
dignitary attending a state funeral. A second waiter presents a menu
with great flourish. Two others, apparently joined at the shoulders,
take my order.

Already drunk at the mere thought of my first cheese in a year—

and soon to discover that I have picked up lactose intolerance along with other native customs—I develop a craving for wine. A fifth waiter passes by, and I call out in Bahasa Indonesia. Caught off-guard, he nearly topples over in his eagerness to stop. He leaps to my table, responding immediately in English. Then, apparently taken as much aback as I am, he stands speechless, blinking at me.

The fifth waiter at the Jakarta Pizza Hut is distressingly perfect. Indonesians tend to be lovely, but his beauty is universal, completely lacking ethnic stamp. He is tall and well built, with luxuriant, blue-black hair and sculpted features. His dazzling smile relaxes into a generous mouth; his dark eyes gleam with what I choose to interpret as sincerity. As conservative in dress as a Connecticut college boy, he is well, yet not overly, groomed—reassuringly unlike the pretty island boys in clicking-heeled shoes who prey on and are preyed upon by foreigners.

> Pizza has made its way onto menus and tables around the world. The most popular pizza topping in Japan is squid, in Australia eggs, and in India pickled ginger.
>
> —LB

Though such smooth beauty does little for me, I am suitably impressed. I explain that I want to order a glass of wine and ask him please to send my waiter.

"Yes," he answers promptly. "A glass of wine. Certainly!" He leaves, glancing back over his shoulder at me. Almost immediately he reappears and places an entire carafe of wine on the table. I am surprised, but a year on the road has taught me not to question any perks along the way. As I thank him, I notice my gestures becoming expansive and more gluttonous.

After a year, the simple act of having wine with a meal is thrilling. The cheap juice enters my system like a fun childhood friend who doesn't really care what's best for me. Once I glance up just as the fifth waiter happens to be passing by. He feels the movement and falters in his path, watching me out of the corner of his eye. Confused, I look away.

A bit later I raise my head to find him facing me, standing perfectly motionless with his arms folded behind his back like every uniformed native in every tropical travel poster. At my gaze he promptly glides forward, asking, "Yes?"

"Oh no, nothing!" I protest, wondering if I had indeed summoned him.

He asks in faltering English what I am reading, and it pleases me that his first question is not where am I from and why am I alone. His name tag reads Sudirman.

"About Bali," I answer, touching my guidebook. "It's where I'm going next."

He steps to my right and picks up the book, his movements respectful yet confident. I wonder if he comes from money. We chat, and as it turns out, he is a student at the National Institute for Hotels & Tourism. This job is his field experience rather than his livelihood. I am somewhat intrigued. Though I attend the occasional expatriate gala event, most of my friends are hungry priests, artists, activists. Sudirman is not the kind of Indonesian I usually meet.

He offers politely to take me sightseeing. I thank him and decline. I have plane reservations for Bali tonight.

"Tonight?" he asks, his eyes widening. "Then please, when you return, to come here—or to my home." He takes out his pen and opens my book. "May I?" he asks, before writing his address on the inside cover.

I am explaining that I do not plan to return, that I hate Jakarta, when the twin waiters appear and stand behind him, clearly impressed by his self-assurance. We are all impressed. They peek over his shoulder and when I laugh, they blush, nodding to me.

Sudirman looks up, smiles, and touches first one and then the other lightly on the cheek. "My friends," he says tenderly, and something in my chest shifts.

He turns back to me, still incredulous at my news. "You don't come *back* from Bali?" he asks, and I nod. He considers this and then makes a gentle suggestion: "I think you had better cancel?" Eyes wide, he nods encouragement. "Yes, *please* to cancel your flight to Bali."

Bali. The place everyone in Indonesia seems to be dreaming

about, travelers and natives alike. I am only passing through Jakarta on my way from one such dream place to another, my loose itinerary based on adding excursions to not-so-well-kept secrets gleaned from the travelers' circuit. What keeps me moving is the belief that the best things in travel are the unexpected treasures that appear (and disappear) along the way—that which can't be planned or held. I tell myself that I don't need Sudirman. I don't need any of his possibilities. I've never before stopped moving for anything or anyone.

I consider the fifth waiter's proposition, anyway, twirling my empty wineglass. I wonder what would happen if I stopped just once. I *wonder*. With all this wine and cheese in my stomach, I feel as warm and relaxed as if Bali were inside me. *Should I cancel?*

Sudirman nods, smiles, waits; and I realize that I spoke out loud.

I have been avoiding local pick-ups, though recently I have been regretting this decision. I was in Central Java during the month of Ramadan, and the entire city sat up every night, gathering at tiny candlelit stalls to watch flickering shadow-puppet plays and wait for the 4 A.M. meal. On every dark street corner Muslims grouped together, murmuring and laughing quietly. Crouched among the *wayang* musicians, sleeping children and their dogs in my lap, I could have fallen easily in love and stayed on, settling into the rhythm of the sleepless city.

I think about rushing back to the guest house tonight before my flight to say goodbye to my Jakarta family: Edina from Berlin and Bud from Portland, whom I keep running into throughout Southeast Asia and who have been feeding me since the robbery. Mary, the beautiful Malaysian anthropologist who brings us treats from embassy fêtes. Rudy, the Sumatran owner, who has been letting me stay at the guest house for free. Later he will take me to the airport, kiss me on both cheeks and the forehead, and say, "You shouldn't trust anyone, even me. You're always welcome. Send a telegram if you run into trouble." I think about arriving to yet another unknown city at night with my bag that never unpacks completely.

I hadn't noticed Sudirman leave, yet suddenly he appears with garlic bread and another carafe of wine. "You have decided?" he asks, putting the food I haven't ordered on the table before me. "You cancel?" We laugh, openly appraising each other, and he nods slowly until I am nodding, too. "Tomorrow and tomorrow," he says with a smile. "Keep canceling."

"O.K.," I say. If I didn't stay for something in Central Java, I decide, I can stay for something, here, now. "I cancel."

He pours the wine. "It is O.K.?" he asks, watching me. "I visit after working tonight?" We both know his question is a formality.

A young, well-dressed couple enters the restaurant, and after excusing himself, Sudirman runs over to shake hands with the man. Immediately another waiter takes the opportunity to refill my glass and ask where I am from, why I am alone. I pay the bill, which consists only of the order taken by the Siamese twins. As I expected, there is no garlic bread, no two carafes of wine.

Sudirman returns and walks me out. "I finish at twelve o'clock," he says quietly, and his words caress the space between us. I feel them like the back of his hand against my cheek. "Don't fall asleep."

Startled at this sudden intimacy, I take a step back. "But I'm exhausted!" I warn him. He smiles, says nothing. "Well," I concede. "You better really show up, then!"

"I will," he promises. "Don't sleep."

At eleven-thirty we are all lounging at the guest house kitchen table, debating the best cities in Asia to receive mail *poste restante*, when Sudirman strides in, immaculate in pressed royal blue corduroys, polished loafers, and a long-sleeved, blue and white tuxedo-style shirt. Gleaming in the light of the dingy kitchen, he is even more than I remember. I realize I hadn't really expected him to come.

"Uh, hi," I say, at a loss.

Placing two large pizzas on the table, he bows to the circle of stunned foreigners and sits down next to me. I feel as if a gentleman caller has wandered into my grandmother's parlor. After a moment he holds out his hand and asks me, "Will you walk?" As we stand up, the group of travelers comes to life, ripping into the pizza boxes with cries of delight.

Edina turns to me, stuffing cheese into her mouth and shaking her head. "There you go again, Faith!" she mumbles between bites. "Just this morning you were broke, hungry, and hating this Jakarta. Now we are all indulging in expensive imported food! How *do* you do it?"

Later, when Sudirman and I return from our walk, I find the kitchen dark, the pizza boxes empty. All that's left on the table is a matchbox with the words *Pizza Hut: Jakarta ★ Singapore ★ Bangkok* emblazoned on the cover—my itinerary in reverse. I smile and turn the matchbox over to find a drawing of a prickly durian fruit on the underside.

Though durian flesh is reportedly rich and intoxicating, its stench is so overpowering that few Westerners dare taste it. There are countless tales of travelers fainting in durian fields or abandoning cars they thought were about to explode because of ripe durian in the trunks. For decades durian was banned from transport ships and airplanes, making it the quintessential Asian fruit, relegated to the shores of its homeland.

For the next three nights Sudirman appears, and for the next three mornings I do as he suggests: keep canceling. Tomorrow and tomorrow. On the fourth night, we tire of these courtly nighttime strolls and grapple together sadly against a bush of night-blooming jasmine. As we press our lips against each other's, I know that Sudirman will come no more. In the morning, I move on, the matchbox my only souvenir.

Faith Adiele's travel essays have appeared in Ploughshares, Ms., Transition, Creative Nonfiction, 4th Genre, *and numerous anthologies. She lives in Iowa City, Iowa, where she is at work on two memoirs, one an account of being the first Black Buddhist nun in Thailand and the other about growing up Nigerian-Scandinavian-American in the rural Northwest.*

TAMARA HOLT

The Language of Taste

Open your mouth to the universe.

THE WORST THING ABOUT EATING GRASSHOPPERS IS THAT THEIR legs get stuck between your teeth. I don't eat insects very often—in fact, I have only tried them once—but I did go back for a second bite. I do, however, make a habit of tasting anything edible, that is, anything that anyone, anywhere in the world, considers edible. It has always been my way of adventuring—taking in, quite literally, all that the world has to offer. "How can you experience another culture without trying its food?" I always say. But it is more the wild woman in me that insists on consuming the exotic, the peculiar, the unidentifiable.

It was an innocent enough idea, in my early youth, when I started to taste the few blocks surrounding my Manhattan home. I sucked pieces of sugar cane down to bare fibers with the shopkeeper at the neighborhood Caribbean market, and crunched whole coffee beans from burlap sacks at Zabar's while my father waited for his to be ground. When I was old enough to ride the subway on my own, I lugged jars of bean paste, preserved vegetables, and cans with vague labels like "Green Jelly" home from Chinatown to sample. But my perverse penchant for trying unknown edibles didn't reach its peak until I started to travel.

I travel alone, I travel dangerously, I stay at hotels with "character" instead of amenities, and I always eat street food. Few things whet my appetite like a line of locals at a steaming pushcart parked on the edge of a dingy side street. I line up with the rest and wait my turn as I try to divine the ingredients of the mystery I am about to consume. Attempts at translation are usually moot, for my fellow foragers tend not to be the types who are instructed in English. And even if they know the basic phrases like "very good" and "you will like," translations for such words as "tripe" or "radish" remain elusive.

> I remember street food in Beijing with pleasure. Cilantro-flavored chilies over steaming noodles on a freezing morning in Sichuan. Hot noodle soup near a frozen canal. *Jian bing*, fried crepes, everywhere. The food was part of a carnival and the carnival was part of why we travel—a joyous celebration of everything out there, strange, odd, weird, and often, unexpectedly, delicious.
>
> —Joan Aragone, "Street Food"

Some of my adventures are less pleasurable than others, but the goal is to taste and I always try at least one bite. I have sampled spongy, greasy, chopped-up protein-of-some-sort, sauced with fiery salsa and wrapped in tortillas on the streets of Oaxaca; gnawed on sticks skewered with tender, salty, I'm-not-sure-what offal in a seaside village in Turkey; and carefully cut away the outer peel of a green- and orange-tinged fruit that I bought off a dusty handkerchief from a sun-worn woman in Cochin, before tasting its acrid flesh.

Most of my epicurean feats, however, are more than worth the risk, as if there are gustatory gods rewarding me for blind faith. My first sip of a syrupy golden-sweet squash purée, served in a half-rinsed half-gourd bowl by a Central Mexican market woman, changed my perception of pumpkin forever. The flavor of the chili-topped pancake I bought on the streets of New Delhi is safely stored in my mind in the spot where I keep memories I can only pray to relive. And few tastes in my life compare with the perfection of an Istanbul street-seller's crisp cucumber, peeled, slit lengthwise, and wiped its whole length with a salt-dipped knife.

These adventures might sound as if I'm dead set on my own demise—taunting my insides to take revenge. But I am not afraid of my stomach. It has only turned on me once and I arm myself with my own recipe for protection. I voyage with a stock of Pepto-Bismol tablets that I munch at intervals throughout the day, and a well-traveled bottle of antibiotics, "just in case." But my basic strategy for staying healthy in places where my concerned friends warn me, "be careful of the food" and "don't drink the water," is to eat yogurt for breakfast and consume alcohol at all other meals. To me, logic prescribes that a beer or two will kill off any pernicious bacteria intent on ruining my trip. I share this advice cautiously, however, for the truth may be that I was born with a stomach of steel.

On one trip, I wandered into a dead end of the crooked maze of homes on the island of Lesbos, when, like an apparition, a stocky Greek grandmother appeared, shrouded in her widow's black dress, carrying a shallow bowl of something that looked like sand. She pushed it toward me as if I knew what to do and I responded with an expression that would say, "What on earth do you want?" in any language. Then she reached her withered fingers into the bowl, tilted her head toward the sky, and crumbled a large pinch of the substance into her wide-open mouth. She smiled, pushed the bowl toward me, and I did the same. It was warm, tender, and fragrantly sweet and worked its way into each tiny crevice of my mouth. I learned later that this was a form of *helva*—a sweetened milk-cooked semolina, fluffed like couscous and served only for festivities or at funerals to mourners at graveside.

I was still savoring its gritty texture and squinting from the sun when the woman disappeared as instantly as she had arrived. Where had she gone? To mourn? To celebrate? To walk the streets like a missionary of taste, offering sacraments to the unenlightened? She just vanished.

She became a prophet, pulled from Greek myth, to reveal to me my most basic truth. The exchange was beautiful and powerful—

communicating without words through the language of food. She made me see that my adventurous eating is not about experiencing local life or daring myself with dangerous feats of feasting. It is about connecting, trusting, sharing, tasting, opening my mind and mouth to the universe and savoring whatever rains in.

Tamara Holt is a freelance food writer, cookbook author, children's food educator, culinary instructor, and former Food Editor of Redbook. *When she is not eating her way around the world, she is scouring markets surrounding her homes in San Francisco and New York.*

On Pleasures Oral

The meal most longed for is
the meal not yet eaten.

LAWRENCE AND I HAD SAMPLED ONLY A SMALL PART OF VENICE when Monica arrived. Disembarking at the Piazza San Marco, we crossed it, noting the Duomo's landmark rotunda, the rows of apostles draped in scaffold and net. We checked into our hotel, the Panada, at five o'clock and had dinner at ten o'clock—a very light supper at the Pescatore Conte.

The next morning dawn awakened us, weaseling its way in through the casements, creeping down draperies, columning them in substance. The scent of baking bread followed the light, then sound—the clatter of pots and pans, of children's voices rising from the street below.

When Monica disembarked, we were seated at a sidewalk cafe on the perimeter of the Piazza San Marco. Across the wide, noon-bright circle of the piazza, she progressed, a scintillating clove-brown figure, an exotic and imperious Cleopatra clad in a saffron blouse and billowing peasant skirt, preceded by a porter carting her enormous black suitcase and a few smaller bags. Her head was uncovered, scarved only in the straight black fall of her hair. She seemed made for the heat. Her Italian movie-star carriage had the usual grand and eye-stopping effect. Pigeons scattered. Heads turned. Men's hands reached involuntarily out toward her as she passed, thumbs and forefingers kissing in empty pinches that would never be consummated.

At that moment, I realized that I loved Monica in the same way that I loved my Barbie dolls as a child, with the passionate attachment one feels toward an ideal shimmering on the distant never-to-be-attained horizon. Men also had this feeling for her.

Lawrence and I pushed back our chairs, threw our napkins down next to our plates and advanced toward her with the well-choreographed precision of two chorus line extras supporting the principal dancer.

She rewarded us with a white flash of smile.

"*Ciao*," she sang out to us. "When did you get here?"

"Last night," we answered in unison.

"Don't you love it?" Monica crooned, echoing the pigeons that cooed, pecked, and preened around our ankles and feet, their plump, feathered bodies pressing carelessly up against us.

"More so now, because you are here," we responded.

"Well, I *have* to get rid of this luggage," she confided with well-practiced urgency. "Then, I will show you *my* Venice."

I've always felt very small next to Monica, small and childlike, like a pawn. My adoration only increases when I see the impact she has on everyone else. On her ample bosom, Lawrence's head had found a place to come, metaphorically, to rest. At least, I hoped it was metaphorical. I watched the two walk, arm-in-arm, ahead of me while I dawdled on bridges, and the chipped, gap-toothed buildings leaned toward us, leering like doddering courtiers drunk with the sunlight.

"Where did you eat last night?" Monica asked as we walked past a series of portside cafes on the Canale Della Giudecca.

"At the Pascatori Conte," Lawrence replied.

"Hmmm," she said thoughtfully as if trying it out in her mind. "I've never eaten there." She paused for a moment considering this. "Well, tonight," she said with a long, slow smile, "we will dine at the Bai Barbacani. It is better than that one, Au Pied de Cochon, in Paris, remember? You will love it. I'll introduce you to Aldo, the owner. I wonder if he will remember me?"

There was no doubt in my mind about this.

We expected other friends to join us in the afternoon, but they arrived exhausted and ill. Dinner for them was out of the question.

Night had pitched its black tent over the city. Monica, in her sunflower-yellow dress gleamed like a beacon beneath the lanterns that lined the narrow alleyways near the canal. On the marled stone walls that rose from the shadows on the opposite bank, small windows opened like the tiny doors in an advent calendar, torch-lit, adventures seeming to smolder within their confines. The entrance to the Bai Barbacani was behind one of these windows.

We crossed a narrow bridge to Calle del Paradiso, on the other side of the canal. At the portals of the Bai Barbacani we were greeted by a slender, tuxedoed waiter who escorted us into the cavelike interior to a round white-clothed table where the candlelight danced, sylphlike, over crystal, china, and silver.

Light flooded over Monica's shoulders pooling gracefully at the juncture of her breasts. Her eyelashes cast shadows on the rise of her cheeks. Lawrence's hair glinted fiery.

Our waiter seemed adequate, but Monica was still restless, her eyes on a tall broad-shouldered man impeccably dressed in a double-breasted blue jacket cut to enhance a narrow waist.

He was making his way across the room, stopping at each of the tables and chatting with guests. His progress was arrested at the table next to ours for he seemed to have found among these diners several dear friends.

"Aldo?" I asked.

"No," said Monica.

"Aldo is not here," she added with just a soupçon of petulance. I noticed that the slightest of pouts had settled upon her carnation-red lips. The restaurant seemed to have changed, to have been rearranged. Gone were the dusty bottles of homemade *fragolino* that Monica had raved about. The broad-shouldered man was laughing, leaning into the table right next to us, ignoring our table completely. He summoned a waiter who disappeared into the back of the restaurant and returned with what must have been a very special bottle of wine. It was uncorked with great ritual. The diner who sampled it nodded his head furiously. The broad-shouldered man squeezed his arm and moved on to us. His dark hair was thin and cut very short. He had eagle-like features. "Welcome to the Bai Barbacani," he said, in musically accented English.

"Where's Aldo?" Monica demanded in response.

"He is gone," said our host.

Monica let him know that Aldo was missed.

"I was here before Aldo," the man replied simply. "I went away and now I am back. Aldo is gone."

He said this with the finality of a man who is used to fitting his confreres with shoes of cement.

"I don't believe you," Monica whispered tauntingly. "I think you have Aldo locked up in the basement."

"So," the man said looking down at Monica, noticing appreciatively the way the darkness gathered at the top of her breasts like a pendant of jet and, sliding between them, disappeared into the soft yellow fabric of her bodice.

He lifted his eyes to us and smiled.

Monica told the man that Aldo had promised her certain secrets—"secret recipes"—when she returned and she wasn't pleased to find him no longer there. Our new host was given to understand that she liked him less.

He asked her, "You don't like me as much?"

Monica shrugged and smiled. "I miss Aldo," she said.

It was a challenge, a gauntlet thrown down. Then it began—the wooing. Perhaps it was the candlelight that bathed everything in a kind of fairy-tale beauty, perhaps it was the desire to best the chivalrous Aldo or maybe it was the Circean net that Monica carried for occasions like this one. Whatever the cause, though the waiter returned and was very solicitous, the man could not seem to stay away from our table.

"Come, come back to the kitchen with me. I can show you how to stir the risotto," he said archly.

We had visions of Monica being abducted into the back, into the restaurant's nether regions, into the basement where Aldo was most certainly buried.

Monica laughed. "Maybe," she said. "Maybe later."

For an appetizer Monica ordered a bowl full of mussels, and our host nearly swallowed his tongue. Piled high on their perfect white china bowl, each glistening shell held the tiny mollusk that has been compared to that most delicate part of a woman's anatomy. Pry open the shell, shut as tight as virgin's thighs, and you feast on the sweet mound of flesh in its own fragrant liquor. Dress them with wine or eat them undressed—either way, to consume them is heaven.

Paulo (by this time we knew his name) leaned over Monica's shoulder and asked, not so innocently, if she'd like him to put a little lemon on them. Monica said "yes," so he called over the waiter who arrived with the proper tools—a silver plate holding a gauze-wrapped half-lemon and a small silver spoon. Paulo expertly disrobed the lemon and took firm hold of the spoon. He very aggressively screwed his small spoon into the lemon, dribbling its juices all over Monica's mussels. Monica watched him. He continued to screw away, eyes upon hers, really building up a sweat in the process. It seemed to go on forever. I was amazed. I'm sure none of us thought there could be that much juice in a single lemon. But Paulo was determined to lemon-up the mussels to Monica's satisfaction or knock himself out trying. It was pathetic.

"Monica," I wanted to plead, "make him stop."

As if reading our minds, Monica finally purred demurely, "That's enough. Thank you." Imaginary handkerchiefs went to three foreheads—Lawrence's, Paulo's, and mine.

I had ordered sweet and sour sardines for an appetizer. I do not want to speculate upon their metaphorical value. Lawrence had ordered mussels as well, but all he got were a few cursory twists of lemon from the waiter.

Monica consumed her mussels with incredible gusto and even offered a few to me, though she knows that I'm allergic to shellfish. It's an allergy I developed recently and one that I never manage to recollect without a puritanical pang.

The appetizers had nearly exhausted us. I wasn't sure we were ready to deal with our entrees. To calm my nerves, I ordered risotto—a sweet pearly mixture, perfectly flavored, designed to comfort the taker. Lawrence had scampi—meaty pink prawns that he sepa-

rated from their wafer-thin jackets of exoskeleton with fingers perfumed in lemon water.

Monica ordered gnocchi, a regional favorite. Satiny black pillows
colored with cuttlefish ink and bathed in a fragrant salmon-red
sauce—before us the simple potato dumplings lay, transformed into
something incredibly sexy.

Round two, I thought. *Victoria's Secret. Frederick's of Hollywood.*

Paulo appeared, again, along with the entrees.

"This is the perfect choice for you," he said to Monica, his hand,
braceleted at the wrist, gesturing toward her plate.

"I love those colors," giggled Monica.

"Come to the kitchen with me," Paulo challenged with a canine
grin. "I will show you how it is done."

Monica laughed, "I'll bet," she said, and bit into one of the little
black pillows. Her sharp teeth cut a tiny half-moon out of one side.
I'd swear Paulo was salivating.

"Do you know," he asked, warming to the subject of food as he
watched Monica eat, "do you know how I like to eat spaghetti?"

"No, how?" asked Monica.

"I float a wooden bowl of spaghetti in my swimming pool." His
large hands placed an imaginary bowl upon the cobalt-blue waters
shimmering in front of him.

"Then I float up to it."

We could now picture him in swim trunks approaching the
spaghetti that bobbed in its big wooden bowl on the water's flickering surface.

"Then, I suck the spaghetti slowly out of the bowl," he said,
looking down at Monica. He was grinning from ear to ear.

"Oh, that sounds wonderful," Monica responded, placing her
napkin beside her plate and gazing up into his dark brown eyes.

"You could try it," he said, raising an eyebrow.

"Do you know what my favorite food is?" Monica countered. "It
is *mascarpone* cheese. Do you know how to make *mascarpone*?"

"Yes," said Paulo. "This cheese takes a long time."

"It does," agreed Monica. "I make fabulous *mascarpone*. I can
teach you to make it my way."

"I would love to make *mascarpone* with you," said Paulo formally. I half-expected him to salute.

"*La vie est belle,*" Monica laughed.

"*Toujours l'amour,*" Paulo chimed back.

The clichés began flying back and forth like shuttlecocks. Paulo would not leave our table. He catered to us to the point of neglect of the rest of his clientele. Diners ordered desserts and after dinner drinks. He ignored them. Regulars paid bills and left the restaurant. He ignored them.

We struggled through apple strudels and tortes and polished things off with homemade *fragolino*, a strawberry liqueur more fragrant, Monica declared, than Aldo's.

"This is my *fragolino*," Paulo said with great pride.

It was like perfume, really, a dark beautiful perfume. We chuckled and whispered that he probably had Aldo locked up in the basement making the stuff. Hours had passed. Candles had burned down to mere stumps. All of the other diners were gone.

"Will you come again, tomorrow night?" Paulo asked Monica, leaning over her chair, his mouth close to her ear.

"No," Monica said, turning her face to his, her nose nearly touching the sharp beak that was his. "No, but I'm here every year."

"Well," he said, as she rose from the table, "you must come again, next year."

He took Monica's arm and escorted her gallantly back to the restaurant's threshold. "I will give you the secret then, to the *fragolino*," Paulo said solemnly, exchanging cards with Monica, promising her the recipe "next year," if she came, just as Aldo once had.

Lawrence and I knew better, of course. We had seen this happen before. We knew that the meal most longed for is the meal not yet eaten. We knew that Paulo's appetite had been aroused. And we knew, for certain, that sometime—long before the promised next year—there'd be a knock on Monica's door, and there he would be—the man with a hunger for *mascarpone*.

Linda Watanabe McFerrin has been traveling since she was two and writing about it since she was six. She is a poet, travel writer, and novelist, who has contributed to numerous publications including the San Francisco Chronicle Magazine, The Washington Post, Modern Bride, *Travelers' Tales, and* Salon.com. *She is the author of the novel* Namako: Sea Cucumber, *and the short story collection,* The Hand of Buddha. *She is a winner of the Katherine Anne Porter Prize for Fiction, and lives in Oakland, California.*

* ⋆ *

Savoring the Trail

Even famished, she relished
the long road ahead.

WHEN I PLANNED MY 2,000-MILE HIKE FROM GEORGIA TO MAINE on the Appalachian Trail, I imagined I'd have a lot of time for Deep Thoughts. Spiritual Experiences. Oneness with Nature. In fact, I soon discovered that walking ten hours a day over mountains with a heavy pack burns a lot of calories—up to 6,000 a day—and it was impossible to carry all the food I needed. Forget dieting—on the Trail it was a daily struggle just to eat enough to keep walking, and I spent much of my time dreaming of food, talking with other hikers about food, or, on good days, eating insanely large amounts of it.

This hunger kicked in early. On the third day of the trip, a fine day in early April, I hiked twelve miles, ending on top of Blood Mountain in Georgia, site of a beautiful view—but even more than the view, I remember the bitten-into apple some dayhiker left on the rocks at the summit. I ate it. A few days later, I ate a series of M&Ms that hikers ahead of me had dropped on the Trail; if, like Hansel and Gretel, the hikers intended the trail of candies to show them the way home, they may still be lost out there. Throughout the trip, I often spied random M&Ms dropped carelessly on the path, and as long as they weren't all rained-on and faded, they were mine. "Never refuse free food" became my motto.

Food on the Trail consisted mostly of things that were cheap, light, and easy to make: *ramen* noodles, macaroni and cheese, rice and beans, oatmeal, instant pudding, and powdered lemonade, plus all the candy bars I could eat. When I ran into other hikers, we reminisced about real food, dreamily composing menus for our first meal back in civilization, swapping recipes for lasagna, fried chicken, and chocolate silk pie, exchanging the locations of our favorite restaurants. In restaurants in Trail towns, we lovingly recounted stories of other meals and looked with envy at the other diners' plates, even when our own were full. At a diner in Atkins, Virginia, waiting for my own food to arrive, I could not stop myself from leaning over and asking a total stranger, "Are you going to eat all that?" and pointing to his massive pile of mashed potatoes swimming in gravy. The customer, a trucker, curved his arms protectively around his plate and declined to answer. At one pizza place, the waitress obligingly gave me, and some other famished hikers, the other customers' untouched leftovers. "I'm just glad it's not going to waste," she said. "Usually we have to throw all this away."

On other visits to towns to resupply, I would easily eat two large pizzas, a pint of Ben and Jerry's Peanut Butter Cup ice cream, a half-gallon of whole milk, and a couple of bananas, and then think, "O.K., that was a nice appetizer, now what's for dinner?" If I reached a resupply town in time for breakfast at the local diner, I'd eat the biggest breakfast they had: six eggs, pancakes, toast, sausage, bacon, hash browns—and a chocolate milkshake. Two hours later I'd return for a big lunch before heading back to the Trail. At times I left all-you-can-eat restaurants in sheer embarrassment after five or six plates of food, only to go straight to the nearest burger joint to scarf down a supersized meal to fill in those empty corners.

At one all-you-can-eat place in Virginia, after eating eight plates of food and drinking a couple of pitchers of iced tea, I headed for the women's room to pee. In the middle of this relaxing interlude, a waitress burst into the room like a detective making a drug bust. She and the other women workers had been watching me eat, most of them eyeing my stick-figure body and making large bets that I was bulimic and right at that moment was vomiting up everything

I had eaten. "Sorry," I said, and described the rigors of my trip. "I'm just peeing. Hey, do you have any more of that blueberry pie?"

At Pine Grove Furnace State Park in Pennsylvania, near the halfway point on the Trail, hikers celebrate their progress by attempting to join the Half-Gallon Club, sponsored by the camp store. To join, you must eat a half-gallon of ice cream in one sitting. Anyone who succeeds gets a small wooden spoon and eternal bragging rights. Those who get sick during or immediately after the event are disqualified. On arriving at the camp store, I checked the logbook to see who had been there ahead of me. Hikers I knew, men much bigger than I, had attempted the Half-Gallon Challenge and failed miserably. "Upchucked," said one entry. "Hurl-o-rama," noted another. "No way," said a third. I ate the ice cream easily, then ordered a cheeseburger and a large order of fries.

By the time I reached Maine, I had walked 1,900 miles and, despite this rigorous calorie-loading plan, had lost all of my body fat, including my breasts and hips; at night, my hips, shoulder blades, elbows, and ankles dug painfully into the hard ground, right through the slight cushion of my sleeping mat. It was already September, and as I huddled in my sleeping bag on below-freezing nights, I lay awake, looking at the stars, fantasizing about drinking cups of melted butter or hot bacon grease. I knew this was, objectively, disgusting, but one day when another hiker carried some butter up from town, I ate a half a stick of it, plain, and felt wonderful. One day I smelled pepperoni in the wind, and a quarter-mile later came across another hiker resting on a fallen log, eating some. He finished just as I walked up, but was kind enough to let me lick the grease out of the package.

Just outside Mahoosuc Notch in Maine, at the end of a long, hard day, I found myself still far from the log lean-to I was heading for. I walked through cold, deserted bogland, keeping a wary eye on the setting sun. I walked and walked, dreaming of the macaroni and cheese I'd make when I got settled. There was no sign of the shelter. I checked and rechecked the map. Could I have passed it?

I could have camped anywhere, but I needed water. The land here was boggy, but the water was all underground, absorbed in peat; none of it was standing and available for my filter.

It grew darker.

I passed a puddle left from the last rainstorm, and thought about camping right there on the Trail, filtering water from the puddle to drink and cook with. I decided to go 100 more yards and if there was no sign of the shelter, I'd turn back and camp.

A spruce grouse, eerily tame, watched me from the deep shade of a nearby tree. These birds don't fly away; they will sometimes let you touch them. "Fool hens," early settlers called them, because they would sit still to be killed. The bird watched me with a measured, meaningful gaze, as if it had a message for me. *You are in trouble,* this one seemed to be saying. *Hungry, tired, and cold. Better camp somewhere before dark.*

Voices drifted through the woods: men. Hikers I knew, or strangers?

Cautiously, I advanced along the Trail. It led to a small cliff, so steep that a rough ladder hewn from young trees had been fastened there.

I climbed stiffly, almost falling because my hands were so cold, and my knees, which I had recently injured, wouldn't bend. At the top, on a little plateau, was the shelter.

It was fully dark now. Dimly, I saw the humped shapes of people snoring in their bags on the sleeping platform of the shelter. Nearby, blue domes of tents glowed and the shadows of hikers I knew, backlit by flashlights, pantomimed sorting gear.

Thank God. My stomach seemed to be touching my backbone. I couldn't find my candle lantern or my flashlight, so I limped down in the dark to the spring, finding it more by the sound and smell of running water than by sight. The water was so cold it made my hands ache. I filled my cooking pot with water; gathered twigs to make a fire; poured macaroni into the pot, cooked it, and added the cheese powder, powdered milk, and a little oil. I dug my spoon in —the only utensil I had, apart from a Swiss Army knife—and took a bite.

The mac and cheese was full of foreign objects. Crunchy, hard, shivering into glassy bits when I chewed. Insects? Ashes? Twigs?

Who cared? It tasted wonderful: hot, cheesy, salty, greasy, filling.

I ate it all, then used my finger to get the last sauce out of the pot.

As I crawled into my sleeping bag, I wondered dreamily what the foreign objects were. Probably bugs: that suspicious glassy crunch of chitinous wings. Well, I'd heard they were a good source of protein, and God knows, I needed all I could get. And at least they were cooked.

It was freezing outside, but I could still taste the cheese, the salt, the oil. The warmth of the noodles spread right through my body. On the way to sleep, I had time for one brief thought: *That was one of the best meals I've ever eaten.*

On the trip, when I was not obsessing about food, wondering what to eat next, or trying to guess how heavy a package of rice and beans was, I did spend many long, quiet days walking alone, with plenty of time to think. I saw bears, a bobcat, and every other animal that inhabits the mountains. I walked through snow, lightning storms, torrential rains, jungle heat, and clear, perfect days. I met many wonderful people, on the Trail and off it. And in the end, I did have deep thoughts, was blessed with spiritual encounters, and I did find a deep oneness with nature: in the end, it was as if all the mountains I walked over became part of me. To this day I carry their vastness, and all the horizons I walked over, inside my body and soul. But I also carry another lesson the Trail taught: context is everything. If you're tired enough, cold enough, and hungry enough, even mac

---

Miracles are unexpected, and that night the freeze-dried mashed potatoes turned out to be a gift to us from heaven. They came with instant gravy, margarine, and freeze-dried beans, and tasted so good that we grew silent, savoring the flavor. There was something overwhelmingly sensual about the taste of meat and grease and salt. We licked our plates; we licked our spoons. We even licked the pot.

"This is the best meal I have ever eaten," Sylvie announced.

"This is better," said Bill, "than real potatoes."

—Tracy Johnston, *Shooting the Boh*

and cheese with bugs in it can be delicious. And to this day, even in the midst of civilized ease and plenty, it's hard for me to see an M&M on the ground without wanting to stop, pick it up, and eat it.

Kelly Winters is a freelance writer whose work has appeared in A Woman's Path *and* Women and Thru-Hiking on the Appalachian Trail. *She is the author of* Side Roads of Long Island *and* Walking Home: A Woman's Pilgrimage on the Appalachian Trail, *and lives in New York.*

PAMELA S. LAIRD

✦ ✦ ✦

The Man Who Has the Garden in Lefkes

A retired restaurateur in Greece still has sizzle.

I SET OUT TO FIND STELIO KALAMARES IN THE HOPE OF FINDING some authentic Greek recipes. I never expected to come away with a recipe for life.

As my husband Mark wrestled our Suzuki Samurai up the steep gravel road through fields of riotous color I was thinking about Stelio. What was so interesting about a retired Greek restaurateur that two carefree young British women would end up spending several days with him? I conjured up a Cary Grantish character living in a Beverly Hills mansion magically transported to the highest peaks of Páros. Just then we crested the hill, and the vivid reds, yellows, and purples of the wildflower fields could no longer hold my gaze as I opted for the long view: the majestic navy waters of the Aegean stretching out to the horizon, interrupted by the silhouettes of the neighboring islands of Antiparos and Náxos.

Mark thought Stelio would not be interested at all in extending his hospitality to us—two married, middle-aged Americans, but he was willing to rent a car for the day anyway, for the adventure of getting out of the tourist areas. "He's playing a numbers game," Mark assured me. "He figures if he entertains enough women, eventually, one of them will sleep with him."

57

That seemed possible. The pair who had urged us to find Stelio, college-aged women from Cheshire, Great Britain, were both gregarious and nubile. It was easy to see why an older man might want to entertain them.

The previous night, we had bumped chairs at a harborside taverna while gingerly feeding shrimp tails to a commune of starving pregnant felines with very sharp claws. "I can never resist a cat in a family way," Joanne laughed, and offered us some local wine from their tin tankard. We spent the rest of the evening sharing stories, relishing the almost-warm spring night, the sound of the waves lapping against the harbor wall just a few feet away, and the company of fellow travelers.

When I mentioned that I was interested in learning more about Greek cooking, they both screamed. From then on they couldn't stop talking about Stelio, a Greek who had lived in London running a successful restaurant and teaching cooking lessons on the BBC, now retired back to his homeland. He had been extraordinarily generous in taking Joanne and Lyndsey in when they mistook his house for a hotel. He had taken them to see his farm on Antíparos and fed them his own wines, cheeses, and produce. The only hints of impropriety in their story were references to an extensive collection of erotic art in Stelio's personal bathroom. They had urged us over and over to visit Stelio, mentioning other visitors. Apparently a New England woman had popped over for a visit every day for two weeks.

As we approached a paved intersection, Mark pulled the Samurai over and waved the map at me. "This must be the main road into Lefkes. Turn and go to Lefkes or straight ahead, down to the swimming beach?" This was a cheap trick, as my husband well knows my penchant for the beach, and my disappointment at the small rocky "beaches" of the Cyclades islands we had so far explored. I did falter, but ultimately decided to go for it. I wanted to meet someone real, even if I did have a mythical expectation of him. "Let's go look for Stelio's garden, at least see if we can find it. Lyndsey said we can't miss it if we're on the main road to Lefkes."

Of course, we did miss it and found ourselves turned around at the town square with no way out but the way we came in. Back and forth we drove, slower and slower, back and forth. "Perhaps it's on the other side of town," Mark reasoned. Neither of us had been in Greece long enough yet to conceive that the reason we kept getting turned around at the square was that there was no road out on the other side of Lefkes.

In desperation, we tried going up at a fork in the paved road just before the town square. The road got narrower and narrower, the whitewashed walls of the houses closer and closer, until it ended at a triangular courtyard high above the town square, with only stone stairs descending. We did finally get the Samurai turned around with something like a fifteen-point turn. We both exhaled loud and long when we joined back up to the main paved street, headed out of Lefkes. "This isn't working," we both agreed. Mark parked at the first pullout and we decided to walk back to the square. We were hungry and thirsty and embarrassed: we feared the whole town was talking about the tourists in the Samurai who tried to drive where, obviously, one should not.

Walking along, I noticed a black iron fence and a conspicuously open gate, beckoning us. "This wasn't open when we drove past earlier," Mark confirmed. There was a lush garden, a large aviary in the center, and several private tables separated by dense foliage. Lyndsey's description came back to me. "It looks like a restaurant. Tourists wander in all the time, expecting to be fed, and Stelio often plays along."

We stepped through the gateway, but like deer caught in headlights, we couldn't move. Suddenly my American cultural instincts took over. I couldn't imagine that Stelio truly wanted perfect strangers to stop by uninvited. Mark's scenario, that only good-looking single women are warmly welcomed, began to ring truer in my head. Mark and I exchanged sheepish grins, each waiting for the other to move.

Just then, a door swung open from the adjacent smallish but well kept house we had overlooked on our journeys back and forth just minutes before. A large, fierce-looking Greek woman clad in widow black burst out of the house, halted in front of us, and barked at us in Greek. Having squelched the urge to flee, I managed to squeak out, "Stelio Kalamares?" With a gesture to follow, she led us through the garden to a small table overlooking the sharp drop of the valley wall. Two silver-haired men sat soaking up the still weak afternoon sun, screened from the street by a wall of neon pink geraniums the size of softballs. The woman presented us to the one with wild hair and thick, black-framed glasses.

"Stelio Kalamares?" I wondered out loud.

"How can I help you?" He spoke as he drew himself into a standing position. He was slightly built even with the bulk of a gray sweatshirt. His eyes seemed to stand out from his head at twice their size.

"You are Stelio Kalamares?" I repeated, incredulous. He was nothing whatsoever like my imaginary Stelio. Mark saved me by introducing us and explaining that we had just met some other tourists who insisted we look him up.

"Yes, yes, of course. Please sit down." Stelio spoke the invitation with verve and assured us that wine would be served shortly. He offered us tomatoes and a parmesan-style cheese from the platter he and his guest had been sharing. By the time the ripe tomato and young parmesan flavors mixed in my mouth, I knew we had indeed found the right man.

> I suggest to anyone deciding to travel to befriend a local who will invite you into their home and cook for you. Margarita consoled me with food and also wisdom. Nights when I couldn't sleep for homesickness or altitude sickness I would stay up talking to her. She would respond with ghost stories or stories of how she learned to cook from nuns in Catholic school. I not only received a crash course in Chilean cooking, I learned a fair amount of Chilean history as well. The relationships one makes with the locals and the food make all the difference for a traveler.
> —Heidi Schmaltz, "Life in a Chilean Kitchen"

"Are these from your farm on Antipáros?" I asked just to get him talking so I could hear more of his English, an attractive interplay of Greek and British nuances.

"Yes, yes. How did you know about the farm?" Stelio asked. We told him how we had met Joanne and Lyndsey, and how highly they had spoken of him and his food. He responded with immediate concern that we not ascribe the wrong motives to him. "They showed up here late one night and they had no hotel reservation. What could I do? They are too young to be on their own!" He interrupted himself with the explanation that his other guest did not speak English and he needed to translate what had just transpired. After a few minutes of Greek, he turned to us and introduced his companion. "He is known affectionately as 'The Man Who Fixes the Streets.' He is a good man. You could not pronounce his Greek name."

In acknowledgment, I raised my just-poured glass in the air, nodded, and tasted an astringent white wine with strong pine overtones. "Retsina?" I asked.

"No, no. This I made myself from grapes that grow on my farm near a pine forest," he replied with a bit of bristle to his voice. Retsina or not, it was the perfect accompaniment to the tomatoes and cheese. He shone at this compliment and assured us the tomatoes had been left to ripen on the vine and picked just yesterday.

Freshness of ingredients, simple preparations, and careful matching of flavors, these were Stelio's food themes. With great passion in his voice, he proclaimed the idiocy of complex, sauced dishes like Lobster Thermador. "Boil it and serve it. That's the best thing you can do to a fresh lobster. But you are from California. Do you know the word California means good producer? You must get very good, very fresh produce at home."

Mark and I were charmed by Stelio's knowledge of the root meanings of words, and peppered him with questions. We learned that George means the farmer, Nicholas, the victory of the people, and, of course, that Stelio means stylist, as it comes from sty which traces its origins back to the building of the Parthenon and the style of columns. "Kalamares," we asked in unison, "what does it mean?"

"The son of the man who is yellowish," Stelio replied swiftly and fired at us a question of his own. "I read once that 95 percent of English words have their roots in the Greek language. If so, why do Americans use 'It's all Greek to me' to mean incomprehensible?"

We all laughed.

It was extraordinary how Stelio wove the conversation and between two subjects he was clearly passionate about, food and words, repeatedly brought the conversation back to Mark and me, and all in two languages. He was a three-dimensional conversationalist.

Another Greek guest appeared, and the first one took a hasty leave. Mark whispered to me "perhaps we should go" but Stelio called for more wine and *mezedes* and reassured us by saying it had nothing to do with us, the two men just do not get along so well. Stelio explained that it can be difficult for foreigners to become part of the social fabric of the village. The Man Who Fixes the Streets was originally from the Peloponnese, but he was totally accepted when he married a local woman.

The second man was a Canadian Greek expat who worked the boats all his life, now retired to the hills near Lefkes. Stelio introduced him to us as "The Man Who Owns the Monastery, But Is Himself the Devil." They hissed and spat, bickering in Greek, and we got to see another side of Stelio. Smoothing over the fight with the explanation that it was all in good fun, Stelio continued, "When I moved here, I decided to make a nice garden so that people who passed by would say 'Oh, look, this is good for our village.'"

Stelio offered us some more wine, this time a light fruity red, and motioned for us to taste from the platter of tuna cubes that had been delivered to the table. Given how delicious the simple tomatoes and cheese had been, I lunged in and I was not disappointed. There was nothing fishy tasting to the soft morsel that melted in my mouth. I pleaded for the recipe.

"There isn't a recipe, really. The fish was very fresh...I traded a fisherman friend some produce for it yesterday. Then I brought it home and had it baked in the oven with a little white wine, some oregano, salt and pepper, and olive oil. That's it."

"This is by far the best fish we've tasted so far," I commented and Mark concurred. This engendered a tirade aimed at restaurateurs in

Greece, their use of poor ingredients and methods. Stelio raved on. "They buy tomatoes from *Amsterdam* and use *frozen* fish! They drench everything in cheap oil and salt, then overcook it, and to top it all off, hold it in a steam table!" He taught us to ask to see the fish before it was cooked so that we would know that the fish was both fresh and freshly cooked.

Adopting a professorial tone, he continued his lesson in restaurant management. "It's not the food that really makes a restaurant. The food can be good, or fairly good and if the atmosphere is wonderful, the experience will be perfect. But if the food is perfect and there is no atmosphere…well…" At that moment I was conscious again of the flowers cascading everywhere and delightful songs from the aviary. There's magic in this place, I thought. I nodded encouragement when Stelio confessed he was writing a little book of stories about the people who have come to visit him, the food he serves them, and the conversations. Mark touched my arm and we both stood to leave, fearing that we had overstayed our welcome.

Stelio begged our indulgence and asked us to step into his personal rooms, waving at an entire wall displaying reviews and awards given to his former restaurant in England. "You see. I am Greek so I must exaggerate, but not too much." We read glowing reviews from the London papers, and even one from *The New York Times*. Not too much indeed, I thought.

As Stelio made suggestions of places we should explore with the rest of our day, I wondered when we might encounter the next restroom. Had I one less glass of wine, the story of "The Man Who Has the Garden in Lefkes" would have ended here.

Stelio pointed through his bedroom to the door of his bath. As I was adjusting my clothes, I noticed an attractive marble statue beside the mirror. When I finally registered the shape, I flushed a deep shade of red. Flustered, I turned to go, and caught a glimpse of an erotic photograph that sent a shot of white heat through me. I giggled with the realization that this must be *the* bathroom Joanne and Lyndsey had mentioned. I drew a deep breath and shamelessly pulled the bath curtain aside to get a better view. The photo was actually one of a series; in each there were only two elements, a side view of the trunk of a naked woman and oil being poured onto her belly. The progression was simple; the more oil, the more her back arched. Later I realized that I must have stared at them a long time. Finally my focus began to broaden, and I discovered dozens of pieces of erotic art, statues and paintings and photographs, all of a similar high quality. It was too much. Escape seemed the only option. I fled back to Mark's side and stumbled through my goodbyes.

As we walked back to the car Mark innocently asked if I was feeling O.K. Flushed appearance. Long bathroom stay. Hasty exit. "Is it *turista* or erotica?" I thought. I struggled for words to describe what I was still experiencing.

Though Mark and I talked about Stelio extensively that evening, we had trouble summarizing our experiences, observations, and feelings. Luckily, the next day we found ourselves on a tour of Delos with the New England woman, Stelio's frequent visitor whom the British girls, Joanne and Lyndsey, had described to us at the taverna.

"What is it about Stelio?" I asked her as we rested high on a hillside, seated on benches made of ruins from the fourth century and rubbed our feet, gazing out over more fields of riotous color sprinkled with ancient marble forms.

"Why, his zest, his lust, his passion, of course." The words bubbled out of her. "His passion for food, his passion for language, his passion for sex. Simple pleasures to be sure, but they add up to a full passion for living."

Pamela S. Laird lives with her husband Mark Jacobsen among the redwoods in Sonoma County. They spent five weeks in the Greek Isles with no itinerary, sailing from island to island via ferry and chartered sailboat, following up leads from other travelers. In a former life, she was a consumer marketing consultant. This is her first publication since her days as a journalism student, over twenty years ago.

LAURA HARGER

Blue Crabs

A mother and daughter share
a last meal together.

AS JOURNEYS GO, IT WAS NOT MUCH. ONE HUNDRED THIRTY-FIVE miles down Interstate 95 from Washington, D.C. to Richmond, and then east on 64 until the country ran out of itself at the mouth of the James River, where destroyers and battleships slept at anchor like ghosts in the deepwater harbor of Hampton Roads, outside Norfolk. Into this Navy town—a town of absences and desires, the former of men sailing abroad somewhere, the latter of the women and children they left behind—we arrived one November morning, mother and daughter, Janet and Laurie, thirty-nine and eight, in a dark-green 1972 Ford station wagon.

I refused to enter the small, riverside Pentecostal church that was our destination. We had visited many times before, and today, as always, I perched on a retaining wall behind the church and watched the ship traffic until my mother's errand was finished. Five stories above the calm gray water, more like a lake than a moving river, a midshipman hosed down the deck of a destroyer. Water sheeted overboard, dissolving into mist before it hit the water. I waved to the sailor, and what I imagined to be his destinations unrolled before me: frozen Aleutians, heat-shimmered Indonesian atolls, fairytale oceanside cities that rose like white cliffs from blue water, that were not, like Norfolk, so choked with anger and longing and grief. The sailor, no doubt bound for somewhere more prosaic, say a routine North Atlantic run, waved back. Inside the church a minister was placing his hands on the back of my mother's neck, and Janet, with eleven weeks to live, was dreaming of demons. Next to her was a row of the diseased: a polio victim who had not walked in forty years, a boy born with a misshapen jaw that did not allow him to talk or chew, and others whose illnesses were still invisible, tucked away under their skins, and together they prayed for what the doomed always pray for and never receive — mercy and grace, in a city built for war.

As the last year of her life unrolled, Janet had descended from the ordinary treatments (radiation, interferon) to the experimental (cobalt) to the unusual (herbalism, yoga, tinctures of fish oils, essences of bone and flowers, the whole polymorphous menu of 1970s alternative medicine). One night a few weeks earlier, an elderly German hypnotherapist, skeletal in her black batik gown, had visited Janet and hypnotized her in the cold, dark garden while I watched from my window. The German bent over my mother like a crow, like a witch over her pot, and I began to fear for my mother. I yelled at them from the window, but Janet did not hear me; she was already asleep.

The service was over, and my mother stood in a crowd on the church's front steps. She looked pretty that day, in a brown-print dress whose high waist hid her stomach, swollen as if by pregnancy where the cancer had eaten her abdominal muscles. Janet shaded her eyes and searched the riverbank, and I ran to her and took her hand, trying to guide her to the parking lot.

"Wouldn't you like to stay to lunch, Janet?" the minister, an elderly black man, asked from the top step. He released the hand of the person he'd been talking to — the boy with the deformed jaw — and put his hand on Janet's shoulder. "If your little chaperone will permit it," he said affably. I glared at that hand and tugged at my mother.

"Stop that, Laurie," my mother said, and released my hand. "I'd love to, but today's not the day."

"We hope to see you inside someday, Laurie," the minister said to me. He bent down stiffly, his hands on his knees, into kid airspace. "I don't think you've ever seen our playroom. Brian could show it to you," he said, indicating the little boy beside him.

Brian smiled tentatively. I knitted my forehead and eyed the boy's collapsed face. Then I turned away; he had nothing to do with me or my mother. "Can we go, Mom?"

In the car Janet said, "These are very nice people." She tugged the seatbelt sharply across my waist. "I don't know why you're always such a little beast."

"I'm not," I said, but the image appealed to me: I imagined myself as a small, quick animal, protected by thick fur and armed with sharp claws. "I want lunch," I told her.

Janet sighed, leaning over awkwardly to clip my belt shut. "You won't come indoors, you won't say hello to people, the only time I ever got you to sit down in service you sat there and hummed the whole time." I stayed quiet: it was all true. Also I had ripped pages out of the hymnal, kicked the pew in front of ours, stared at the ceiling when the minister asked us to bow our heads, and asked the lady next to us if the Doxology was about dogs. I didn't believe in God. Nor, until recently, had Janet. When Jessica Epstein, my best friend in first grade, had mentioned God to me, I went home and asked my mother what the word meant. "God is a nice person, like Santa Claus or somebody in a book," Janet had explained. "He's made up."

Janet closed my door and walked stiffly around the Ford's hood to her own side. I noticed the gray that was coming into her hair, veiling the top of her head, and I twisted around for a last look at the Navy boats. Snow had just begun to fall, and it clouded the river; I couldn't see anything. "I want to go to McDonald's," I said when Janet opened her door. In the past few months I had begun insisting on things from her. If I wanted to make cookies, she had to make them with me. If I didn't want to go outdoors or go to sleep, she had to sit and read to me. The more she faded away from me, into the dark garden of the crows and the witches, into the crowds of supplicants at deaf old God's altar, the more I demanded, the more panicked and cranky I became. I'm cold, I need to go to the bathroom, I want to go for a ride. Talk to me, feed me, stay here.

"I want two hamburgers, and a chocolate shake, and an apple pie, and—"

"Don't start with me, Laurie," she said, turning out of the parking lot and into the dead Sunday morning streets. The infant snowflakes hit the windshield and dissolved into tiny rivulets. She turned on the wipers, and they clopped sadly back and forth across the glass. Over their beats she began to talk as she often did on drives back to Washington: as if she was alone. "I've gotten away from my roots, I realize that now," she said. "I forgot God."

"I want fries, too."

Janet nodded, but she wasn't answering me. "God judges forgetfulness. You'll understand that someday." She gripped the wheel tightly as we turned onto the bridge over the James and both banks vanished in a blur of snow fog. The water was white-gray below us and the sky white-gray above us. We were the only car on the road. "I was saved when I was just about your age. My grandmother had me baptized in the river. I bless her for that now."

There was a handful of change, for the tolls, in the open ashtray of the dash. I pulled out a handful and began to chuck quarters onto the floor. "God's like Santa Claus," I said cruelly. "You told me."

"When they put me under the water, I was happier than I've ever been since."

I aimed a quarter at her nyloned right calf. "You're lying," I said absently. "You don't believe in God." I settled back into my seat, about to close my eyes, but her slap, fast and hard against my cheek, set me upright again.

"Don't you ever say that," Janet said, her eyes full on me. I gathered up the rest of the change from my lap and threw it at her with both hands. "You lie," I said again, and she hit me across the top of the head this time. The Ford was fishtailing then, skidding in a lazy half-circle until it came to rest with its back wheels on the bridge's empty east sidewalk.

"Oh, my God," Janet said, and opened her door. She leaned over and I heard her retch and the silver sound of change spilling from her lap onto the road.

"Mom?" I unclipped my belt and scrambled over the seat toward her. I took her right shoulder in both hands and pulled her back as hard as I could. We fell together, half-lying across the Ford's wide front seat. I looked at her face, under the crook of my arm. There was a streak of bloody vomit across her chin and more on the flowers of her dress. I closed my eyes, and such a strange thought came: she is going to die. Somewhere far north of us, the hypnotist in our garden nodded and smiled encouragingly, flapping her black batik wings. The old minister on the church steps invited us inside, holding open the door of his red-brick sanctuary. I moved down until I could put my head on her shoulder. I hoped we would fall asleep together.

But Janet sat up after a minute and looked in the rearview mirror, wiping her chin with the back of her hand. "We were going to have lunch," she said.

There were fresh flowers on the table and fruitwood logs in the fireplace. The inn was a stylish ersatz Colonial building outside Fredericksburg, overlooking the Civil War battlefield, and its hostess was visibly unnerved by Janet's disarranged manner and the dark streak on her chin. We were the only ones in the dining room, and we sat silently on the same side of a big table, watching snow cover the pasture outside a huge picture window. "I haven't been here in a long time," my mother said.

The red-aproned waitress came in with menus and read off the specials in a skeptical voice that plainly said she would go through the motions with us, but no more. She did not offer Janet a wine list.

"We have a Thanksgiving menu," she said. "It's turkey with chanterelles and white truffles."

"I don't like truffles," I said, although I had no idea what they were.

"No, no," my mother said, resting her head in one hand and looking up sideways at the waitress. "That's not what we want."

"We have trout amandine and blue crabs, too. The last of the season."

"I don't like trout," I said.

"No trout," said my mother. "A dozen crabs, please."

"I don't want them," I said, but the waitress was already leaving the room. I kicked unhappily at the table legs.

"You'll like them, sweetie," my mother said. While we were waiting, we fell asleep, me leaning against Janet, Janet with her head on her folded arms. Outside the window the snow sifted down on the battlefield, and on the hearth the fire talked to itself and made sweet smoke. The waitress woke us by thumping down the platter of steamed crabs. "I'll get you some coffee, ma'am," she said, and tied a little paper apron around my neck, plainly not trusting Janet to manage the job. She armed me with a nutcracker and a little wooden mallet, and I looked at the platter miserably. The crabs lay in a tangle of scarlet claws, encrusted with salt and red pepper, expensive and out of season and horrifying. They were fat with autumn roe, and it oozed out of the plates of their bellies. The waitress picked out a little one and laid it on a square of paper before me. She patted me on the head and left.

I prodded one with my mallet. "What do you do with them?"

My mother picked up the crab and turned it over. "They have a pull tab. Like cans of Coke." She pushed the end of her butter knife under the belly tab, lifted it, and broke off the creature's top shell.

I leaned against her and looked down into the crab. A gray and yellow mass of lungs and roe steamed there. "The good stuff is underneath," said Janet, scraping the entrails onto the paper. She snapped the crab's body in half, pulled out a lump of backfin meat, and held it out to me. "Open your mouth."

I closed my eyes. There was the sting of pepper, the bitter edge of the thing's guts, and below that, an incredible flavor, seawater made into flesh, delicate and complicated and completely new. I opened my eyes and pried into the broken carcass for more.

"You like it?" Janet asked, and I nodded. She showed me how to crack the big front claws and prospect inside them with a fork tine to extract the claw meat. She showed me how to suck the fine shreds of meat out of the smaller claws, moving her teeth down a claw as if drawing something out of a straw. After I finished my crab, I went on to another, and another, reducing the platter to a heap of shells and entrails. Red pepper got into my hair and shell bits stuck to my sleeves. When I couldn't open a crab, I silently passed it to Janet, who smashed it with her mallet and passed it back.

I glanced up once at my mother. Janet leaned back in her chair, watching me without smiling. "You didn't eat," I accused her.

"Can't, Laurie," my mother said. "You eat for me." I nodded— O.K.—and plucked a secondary claw off another crab. I sucked the sweet meat slowly, watching the early snow pile up on the windowsill and on the battlefield below, watching Janet fold her arms on the white tablecloth and sink slowly back into sleep.

You never get all the way home from some journeys. Twenty-four years have passed since she died, but I remain with Janet in many places: outside a sad Navy-town church, on a snow-covered bridge above the James River, in a dark garden, and at a strange and solitary lunch where she fed me for the last time, and taught me to eat, and live, without her. I think we're still driving together, somewhere on a stretch of southern Virginia highway, although by now the church is gone, and the inn is gone, and suburban ranch houses have crept right to the borders of the battlefield. I know; I've gone to look. And I wondered then about journeys, and whether they can make a ghost of you.

But a few weeks ago, I brought crabs home for supper. They weren't the crabs I knew—here in California you can buy only wide-bodied, long-legged Dungeness crabs, not the small, delicate blues of the East Coast. The Dungeness is hardier, meatier, and puts up far more resistance to hammer and pick. The cold fast currents and stony shores of the Pacific demand toughness; there's no sweet, rocking, warm Chesapeake for the crabs to hide in here. And I laid one, boiled to a brilliant Golden Gate orange, on the counter before my West Coast-raised husband, who regarded it with mystification: "What do you do with them?" I turned it over: different, but the same. I flicked the familiar belly tab up for him, pulled the creature in half, and placed a lump of meat on his tongue and one on my own. The same flavor, yes—sweet and bitter, sugar and salt, the taste of tears and seas and memory.

Laura Harger grew up on the East Coast and received her MFA from the Iowa Writers' Workshop. She is the author of Lonely Planet's Washington, DC, *and is a senior editor at the University of California Press.*

PART TWO

EPICURIOUS

A Second Helping

*In the company of strangers they discover friendship,
food, and hidden glimpses of identity.*

"HE NEVER EVEN TOUCHED MY HAND!" SERAFINA MOANED LATER.
"Even when we danced he kept his distance."

"I wouldn't let Noureddine touch mine," I said, already
depressed. After dinner they had taken us to a large nightclub in
the new part of town. Noureddine was surprisingly light on his feet
and he pulled me energetically around the floor while I looked
yearningly at Taeb. I wasn't positive we had paired off, but if we
had, I'd lost.

"And he insisted on sitting out all the slow dances," Serafina
continued, ignoring my comment. "The best-looking man I've
seen since I left home and his idea of a good time is the twist!"

"Eight hours ago," I reminded her, "you were terrified that he
wanted your body. Now you're terrified that he doesn't."

Serafina was still shaking her head. "Coming here," she said
darkly, "may have been a mistake."

The next night Noureddine took us to his mother's house.
Orange blossoms gleamed silver in the garden, capturing the
moonlight as we passed. The air was heavy with perfume, and bees
throbbed in their hives. Noureddine bent to remove his shoes, his
bulk filling the small entrance, and then led us into a dark, low-

ceilinged room. Carpets were everywhere: scattered on the floor, tacked onto the walls, thrown over the furniture. In the center stood Noureddine's mother, veiled from head to toe, her hands together in greeting. As I looked into her eyes I felt I was stepping backward a hundred years.

Later Noureddine told me that his mother couldn't read, and I tried to imagine what it was like for an engineer who spoke three languages to have an illiterate parent. I couldn't, but just the sight of this mysterious woman made me feel awkward and tongue-tied. Then Noureddine's sister bounded into the room wearing a straight navy skirt and a white silk blouse and rescued us. "Mina teaches at the university," Noureddine managed to say before she took over, asking where we had been, where we were going, and why we had come to Tunis.

As she talked, her mother was setting platters of food on a round, low table in the corner. There were shiny beets the color of garnets and grated carrots perfumed with orange-flower water. Cucumbers were dotted with olives, oranges sprinkled with rosewater. The food glistened. As their mother left the room Noureddine and Mina began helping themselves, using their fingers to pick up the food.

"Will you be offended," asked Mina in her lilting voice, "if I ask about your backgrounds?"

I wondered if I should say that I was Jewish. I had a quick fantasy that they would all leap up, turn the table over, and demand that I leave the house. But Mina just nodded graciously and said, "Tunis has been home to many Jews." She turned to Serafina.

"It is unusual, is it not, for a white woman and a brown one to be friends in America?" asked Mina.

"No," I said.

"Yes," said Serafina simultaneously, "it is."

We fell silent again as Noureddine's mother reappeared with a large loaf of bread. Taeb tore off a piece and dipped it into the spicy green peppers mixed with tomatoes. Serafina imitated him, but when she ripped the bread from the loaf and dipped it into the rich eggplant salad the gesture suddenly became seductive. She licked her fingers.

"Attention!" said Noureddine. "This is only the first course." And he began telling us about the agriculture of Tunisia. By the time he got to annual date production I was having trouble stifling my laughter. I caught Serafina's eye. "Stop it!" she said, and then we both exploded in uncontrollable waves of mirth. There was a tense moment and then the corners of Mina's mouth turned up, she giggled too, and it was all right.

We couldn't eat more.

We did.

Platters came and went at a dreamlike pace. Each seemed to leave the table as full as it had arrived and I wondered what was going to happen to the leftovers.

The *pièce de résistance* appeared, a triumphant pyramid of grain, fish, and spices large enough to feed a small city. Noureddine held up his right hand. "I will show you the proper way to eat couscous," he said, dipping delicately into the platter. He brought some of the grains toward him, rolling as he pulled, and then popped the ball into his mouth. "You will notice," he said, "that my fingers do not touch my mouth. Now you try."

I tried. The grains went spinning out between my fingers and all I got was a handful of air. "Try again," he insisted. This time I got three grains of couscous and a piece of fish. "Better," said Noureddine, "but you touched your mouth. Again."

I kept trying, forgetting how full I was. I finally mastered the technique, but by then Serafina was urging Taeb to teach her to eat, inching closer for the lesson. As he showed her how to grasp the grains, she leaned against him. He edged away. But once he unconsciously took his fingers and brushed some couscous from her cheek, then snatched them back as if her skin were on fire.

We had intended to spend a few days in Tunis before going on to Algiers and Meknes. But more than a week had passed and neither of us had mentioned leaving. The boys were always with us and our bones seemed to be filled with sweet Tunisian honey that slowed us down, changed our rhythm.

We walked and danced. We spent twilight sipping cool lemon-

ade on the terrace of the Café de Paris and in the evenings we ate
spicy *tajines* and grilled *merguez* sausages. We wandered through the
alleys of the medina, catching glimpses of fountains playing in sun-
drenched courtyards. Occasionally Noureddine took my hand, like
a brother or a cousin. And then there was Taeb.

We both dreamed about him. Serafina did more than that, but he
hardly seemed to notice. "All this time and we're still just friends,"
she fumed. "I wish I understood this country."

Then Noureddine started talking about driving down the coast
to Sousse and Mahdia and Sfax. "You must see the Great Mosque,"
he insisted. "It was built in 851. And the Ribat, a masterpiece of
Islamic architecture, which is even older."

"How exciting," said Serafina, barely repressing a yawn.

"No more monuments, please," I demurred.

It was Taeb who insisted. "The Sahel is more than monuments," he
said. "The beaches are the most beautiful in the world. We'll be back
in time for my sister's wedding next week." And then he clinched it
by putting his hand on Serafina's arm and urging, "Please come."

The road south was empty, or I remember it that way, lined with
tall palm trees. Donkeys grazed along the side, looking up, ears twitch-
ing, as we passed. An occasional dromedary ambled into the road so
that Taeb had to honk impatiently to get the rider to move over.

After a few hours we stopped to swim. There was nobody on the
beach and as we separated to put on our bathing suits, I had a sudden moment of modesty, remembering that the boys had never seen
us dressed in less than skirts and blouses. Looking at Serafina's full
breasts and tiny waist I regretted every bite of couscous. Indeed,
both boys gasped when they saw her.

Later we pulled off the road at a little whitewashed shack with
blue awnings. We were the only guests, and the proprietor rushed
about pulling chairs up to a table. There was a negotiation—
Noureddine, of course, did the talking—and then the man left.
We could hear him in the kitchen, rustling about and talking to
the cook.

I was surprised when a bottle of rosé wine appeared on the table;

in Tunis the boys had not touched alcohol. It was crisp, icy cold, and heavy in the mouth. With the first bottle we ate peppered almonds and olives from the trees growing all around us. We had a second bottle with the *mechouia*, the spicy mixture of charcoal-roasted chilies and tomatoes. By the time we got to the grilled fish I could feel my cheeks start to flush. Across the table Taeb was feeding dates to Serafina, slowly, with his fingers. Then she picked up a slice of watermelon—the fruit was almost unbearably sweet—and devoured it with sharp, delicate little bites. Taeb watched so intently that for the first time she was the one who looked away.

It was almost dark when we checked into our hotel, a few simple bungalows scattered between palm trees on the sand. Serafina hummed quietly to herself as she undressed, and I felt sad and empty. We didn't talk much. I woke up once in the middle of the night and thought Serafina was not in her bed. But she was there in the morning, fast asleep. Had I been dreaming?

We had rolls and coffee in the hotel and then went out to the beach, which was as fine as they had said it would be. It was empty and quiet. The sea was very blue and the sun was bright but not too hot. Fishing boats drifted along the horizon. We lay on blankets for a while and then Taeb jumped up and said he was going to visit his aunt. Noureddine said he would go along to show respect.

"You didn't say you had an aunt here," said Serafina.

"Tunisians have family everywhere," he replied. "Coming?"

I would have gone, of course, if Serafina had, but she wouldn't go. Was this a lover's dance? I couldn't tell. She went back to her book and I rolled over, looked lazily at the water, and went to sleep.

I woke up famished. But as we walked along the sea road to town I grew skittish; we were unaccustomed to being alone in Tunisia. "It seems awfully empty," I said. "It doesn't look as if a single tourist has ever been here."

"Ohh," mocked Serafina, "scary." We reached the edge of the town and peered at the menus posted in the café windows. Not one was translated.

"It doesn't matter," she said, marching toward a little café with strips of red, white, and blue plastic hanging across the door. We sat beneath an awning at an outside table and Serafina ordered an omelet, salad, and a glass of wine.

The waiter looked worried. In halting French he said something about flies, insects, the need to move indoors. "It will be stifling in there," said Serafina, "we're not moving. We don't mind a few flies."

The man nodded and went away. Ten minutes went by. Twenty. Forty. Nothing arrived. We called the man out and he said yes, yes, the food would arrive any minute. "And the wine," I said, "don't forget the wine."

He nodded and went back inside. Another half hour passed. Nothing happened. "This is ridiculous!" said Serafina. "I feel like I'm waiting for Godot."

She went off to find the waiter and came back with a quizzical expression on her face. "They've all gone home," she said, "and the door's locked. We're the only people here. What do you think happened?"

"It is not a mystery," said Taeb when we told him later. We were having dinner at the shack on the beach, eating ravenously. He was sipping wine. "This is not Tunis. This

---

I walk the streets among Spaniards out for *paseo*. Darkness falls and I stop in a bar whose doors stand open to the salt air. A white-haired man talks with a mouthful of olives to the bartender. They both listen patiently as I explain that I've forgotten the name of the restaurant where I'm to meet my group for dinner...

"Let us feed you," says the man with olives in his mouth.

"Yes, a nice *tapa de tortilla*," the bartender says.

I'm hungry and tired, and I let the bartender put a plate of olives in front of me. This would feel different in the States: a lone woman at a bar. But Spanish *tapa* bars, the center of social life, feel embracing rather than alienating. Soon a *tortilla*—a potato omelet— and a frosty beer arrive, and I am warmed by the food and the soft murmur of conversations around me, the feeling of being a part of this moment in this bar in Santander.

—Lucy McCauley,
"Lost in Spain"

is a small town where Arab women do not sit outside by themselves drinking wine!"

"But we aren't Arab women," Serafina said.

Taeb gave Serafina a sidelong glance. "Really?" he asked politely.

I looked at Serafina, suddenly realizing what they had been seeing all along: Her shiny dark hair and honey-colored skin.

"But I'm not!" she said.

"I know," said Taeb, in the soothing voice you use to calm a fractious child. "I know." He started peeling oranges and feeding the sections to Serafina, who took them delicately with her teeth, like a cat. The back of my neck prickled; Taeb's stillness had disappeared.

We went back to the bungalow and Serafina spent a long time at the sink, washing her face. "They think you are here to discover your roots," I said. "They think you don't know it." She bent to rinse off the soap. She dried her face, muffling it in the thickness of the towel.

A few days later Taeb's sister Fatima was married. The wedding was held in a large, fragrant Tunisian garden so filled with flowers it looked tropical. The men in their Western suits were somber spots of darkness, but all the women, even Mina, were arrayed in long silk robes and colorful veils.

The men left before the bride was carried into the garden on a high palanquin, wrapped in silks and holding her henna-dyed palms before her face. All we could see were her eyes, heavily rimmed in kohl. As she sat on a dais, all the women in the garden began to ululate, the sound bursting from their vibrating throats as if their hearts were speaking. The primal sound, agony and approval, floated up into the air and over the garden wall.

The music began and the women started to dance with wild, sexy movements, swinging their hips and shaking their breasts with a freedom they never displayed in mixed company. It was lovely. Tiny cakes were served, punctuated by laughter, music, and songs. It went on for hours and toward the end I allowed myself to be pulled into the dance. It was an odd feeling, knowing that no men were watching. I was just relaxing into the rhythm when I noticed that Serafina had disappeared.

In a panic I went rushing from table to table, searching for her. She was not at any of them. She was not dancing. Finally I saw a knot of women in the farthest corner of the garden. There she was, very still, surrounded by a dozen women talking in high, animated voices. Mina was in the circle too, holding a garment over Serafina's head as if she were a child about to dress a doll.

Mina pulled the long silk red robe over Serafina's short Western dress. She covered her hair with a silver-embroidered silk scarf, pulling the ends so that they fell across her shoulders. She looped silver chains around her neck and began to outline her eyes in kohl. I watched as this new, softer woman emerged. Serafina looked as if she belonged in the garden. I was alone.

A few moments later the groom came to claim his bride, followed by the rest of the men. Taeb was taller than the others so I could see his eyes light up when they landed on Serafina. Serafina saw it too. Her mouth twisted and she began pulling off the costume. By the time Taeb had worked his way to her side she was herself again, but for her kohl-rimmed eyes.

The party was over. The bride was carried out and everybody made suggestive jokes about the wedding night. The honeymoon would start tomorrow. Serafina and I stood outside the garden with Taeb and Noureddine, wondering what to do with ourselves. It was too early for bed. "Let's go to the movies," Noureddine suggested, "there's a new James Bond."

We went down the hill to the huge new cinema on the Avenue Habib Bourguiba. We settled into plush seats in the balcony. The ads were already playing, and on the screen some boys skateboarded dangerously along a California sidewalk holding up bottles of Coke. Taeb must have tried to take Serafina's hand because I felt the jerk of her body as she pulled away. Then the camera tilted up to the San Francisco skyline and I suddenly wished I had a bucket of popcorn on my lap and that I could go outside and find that all the cars were Fords.

★

Two days later we took a plane to Algiers. It was clearly time to go. Taeb said nothing, but was wearing his most intense look, as if he were a hungry man who had been shown a feast. He kissed Serafina gently, one cheek, then the other, then back to the first. Noureddine looked rumpled and miserable. "Why are you leaving?" he cried, as if his generosity had failed and it was somehow his fault.

I threw my arms around him, grateful and sorry. "You were right," I whispered in his ear. "Once you get to know Tunis it is impossible to leave." And then I boarded the plane.

Serafina immediately ordered a bottle of wine. "I feel as if I am waking up from some very strange dream," she said. "In Algiers it's just going to be us, okay? No more men."

"Fine with me," I replied.

But in less than an hour we got off the plane to find a tall dark Tunisian named Dris waiting on the runway. "I am a friend of Noureddine's," he said. "He asked me to take care of you while you are in Algiers. This is a dangerous city."

Ruth Reichl is the former food critic for The New York Times *and is currently the editor of* Gourmet *and* The Modern Library Food *series. She is the author of* Let Them Eat Apples *and* Tender at the Bone, *from which this story was excerpted.*

Sampling
La Vie Provençale

They say "It's never too late," because it's true.

I FOLLOW MY HOST DOWN A NARROW DIRT PATH BEHIND THE Mediterranean-style villa into a garden that overlooks the city of Nîmes in Provence. We pause in front of a small lemon tree with yellowing leaves. He fingers the wrinkled surface of an undersized, deep-green lemon, like a father caressing the cheek of a small child. "Not a good year *pour les citrons*," he says. The callouses on his fingers, dirt lodged under broken nails, and tanned, muscled forearms are evidence of an intimate connection to this land.

I barely know sixty-five-year-old Paul Mure. Only a few hours ago I was sitting on a bus on my way to spend a week in the home of a non-English speaking French family—my long-held dream of a junior semester abroad. Except I have just turned fifty-nine years old. And I've signed up instead for a week-long homestay offered by Elderhostel educational travel programs.

Doubts crowded my mind as the bus approached Nîmes. With what kind of family will I be paired? Will my mostly academic French fall short? What if I'm too old for what is traditionally a college-age adventure? The conventional tour packages I rejected suddenly seemed more palatable. Thankfully, the panic subsided as soon as Paul's sixty-one-year-old wife Colette, a short, buxom redhead with a take-charge demeanor, met me at the bus and planted the traditional welcome kiss on both my cheeks.

Now, as I continue to trail my tall host under exotic trees of cypress, olive, fig, and almond, his gentle manner reassures me. *"Vous parlez bien le français,"* Paul says.

We stop in front of a tree with a fruit he identifies as *arbousier*. He explains that the tree, and many of the other plants I encounter for the first time, grow only in the dry, stony soil of Nîmes or the marshy wetlands of the Camargue on the nearby Rhône River delta. "Three generations of my family have worked this land."

I awake mornings to an intoxicating mélange of fragrances from vines of muscat grapes, patches of rosemary, thyme, and marjoram, iris and *arbousier* blossoms that drift through my open window. Quite a contrast to a stuffy, air-conditioned hotel room.

When I climb the stairs to the kitchen, I am surprised to find Colette in faded, flannel jumpsuit pajamas and bare feet. She tells me that Paul, an early riser, has already driven to town to tinker around the auto repair garage he once owned. We sit down to an array of cereal boxes, a pitcher of what looks like heavy cream, a few hunks of leftover baguette for toast, a bowl of bananas, pears, and grapes, and a pot of fresh-brewed coffee. *"Vous servez-vous,"* she says, motioning for me to help myself.

A typical morning of errands takes us first to the nearby bakery for the day's customary fresh-baked baguette and a chat with the owner. Colette confides that it would be more convenient to buy her bread in the newly opened bakery at the chain supermarket. "But that would be disloyal," she says. "We've been coming here for thirty-six years."

Next we head to one of Nîmes's outdoor markets where I am captivated by an array of locally grown produce: more than ten varieties of mushrooms; beans in cranberry red-and-white striped shells; plump, irregularly-shaped orange and yellow squashes, some slit to reveal a thick, velvety flesh; crisp, lush salad greens minus the brown spots, limp leaves, or dry, shriveled edges I find in my local supermarket. Their perfection reminds me of a Cézanne still life.

"C'est tout naturel," Colette emphasizes. She tells me of her

opposition to gene-altered food products, and, as I gaze around me, I understand for the first time France's reluctance to import farm produce from the United States.

I am intrigued when Colette informs me on laundry day that dryers are *pas naturel* so she doesn't own one. Instead, we spend an hour draping several loads of machine-washed clothes to dry on wooden racks that litter the back terrace. Among them are the Mure's twenty-four-year-old bachelor son's shirts. Colette describes his once-a-week visits to pick up the clean and drop off another batch of dirty ones, and we laugh when I tell her it's the same for American moms. In this momentary suspension of our French and American identities, I feel a strong connection to my hostess as simply a woman and mother. That night, I hold my nightgown to my nose and inhale the fruity, herbal bouquet of the Mures' garden.

Colette's *au naturel* anthem echoes throughout the kitchen. I watch with envy as she combines the magical ingredients from the market with those from Paul's garden, throws in some leftovers from the refrigerator and creates, without a printed recipe, a simple but savory meal. Mushrooms, sauteed lightly in sunflower butter and seasoned with fresh parsley and dried garden herbs. A sage-stuffed pork roast whose day-old scraps join with stale baguette crumbs for reincarnation as a filling in plump, home-grown tomatoes. I cringe recalling the perfectly edible leftovers I routinely toss in my garbage disposal.

When my turn to cook comes later in the week, I dispense with my recipe from home and follow her lead. I improvise a casserole dish using crushed herbs from the garden, day-old chunks of baguette, fresh brown-shelled eggs, leftover appetizer *saucisson* (a salami-like meat), and cheese. In the absence of a microwave, which also violates Colette's *au naturel* code, I bake it the long way in the oven. How pleased I am when both my hosts ask for second helpings.

But what I treasure most about mealtime in the Mure household has more to do with ambiance than food. Despite schedules cluttered with the maintenance of three separate properties, fitness classes, and the ups and downs of three adult children and five grandsons, these two retirees manage to reunite back home in the middle of every day for a four-course, aperitif-to-dessert, sit-down dinner that averages two hours. Not like at home, I think, where brown-bag lunches on the run and carry-out Chinese dinners rule.

The week's mild, late summer weather permits us to dine on the second-story back terrace overlooking lush green tree-tops punctuated by red and purple berries. Three or four glasses of wine, leaves rustling in the warm breeze, and the melodic trills of birds lull the senses. One day we peruse each other's family photos, "oohing" and "aahing" over our handsome progeny. On another, we discuss the politics of European unity and my hosts tell me they are against the French franc's replace-ment by the Euro. "We fear losing our *identité nationale*," they explain. Refrains of Beethoven or Mozart from the living room stereo modu-late these discussions. I mull over how I can transplant this aura of ease and graciousness to time-pressured mealtimes at home.

Each night before I turn off the bedroom lamp, my eyes fix on a framed black-and-white photograph of a herd of black bulls flanked by

M ishe, Nora's husband, and Istvan, their adult son, joined us as we took our places at the table. The food appeared attractive with the variety of colors. We began with the deli-cious salad, then I served them each a slice of meat topped with gravy and surrounded by vegeta-bles. There was no conversation during the meal as the effort to chew required all of our atten-tion and energy. "Please pass the bread" were the only words spoken. The bread was delicious and we each consumed several slices, but no one requested seconds of the main course.

After the meal ended they pronounced it tasty and politely thanked me. I remained in their home for two more months but was never again asked to cook.

—Helen Curley,
"Yankee Pot Roast"

two cowboys on horseback wading through a swamp. When I ask my hosts to explain its significance, they tell me the scene is typical of Provence's Camargue, where a special breed of small black bulls raised primarily for sport graze among the marshes and flamingo-filled lagoons of the wetlands. "Colette's father lives there in our second home," Paul says. "As a young man, he belonged to *les guardians*, the order of skilled horsemen who train Camargue bulls for the ring."

At the end of the week, we visit the Mures' white stone hut with bright blue shutters and thatched roof, fashioned in the characteristic style of the *cabanes* that house *les guardians*. Before we enter the house, Paul, who stands level with the triangular-shaped roof, takes my hand and runs it over the coarse reeds called *sagne*, tightly woven in overlapping horizontal rows that slope on both sides toward the ground. He explains that they grow here in the marshes and their sturdiness protects against Provence's often destructive Mistral wind.

Colette's eighty-four-year-old father, Papa Léandre, awaits us inside the compact, dollhouse-size structure that looks as if it belongs in a jungle landscape. His parched, craggy skin has the texture of cured rawhide. "*Moi*, French cowboy," he says, pointing proudly to a picture of himself as a young guardian mounted on a white horse.

Absinthe is an alcoholic drink made with an extract from wormwood. Emerald in color by nature, it is very bitter and therefore traditionally poured over a perforated spoonful of sugar into a glass of water, which turns it an opaque white. Absinthe was once popular among artists and writers (Van Gogh, Baudelaire, and Verlaine) because it was believed to stimulate creativity. Because it's still considered a drug, it is now sold only in Spain, Portugal, and Denmark. Pernod is basically absinthe without the wormwood, and vermouth, taken from the German *wermuth* (wormwood), is actually made from the flower heads of wormwood.

—LB

A few minutes later he takes me on a tour of the yard. He bends over to tug at a brown twig, unearthing a foot-long stretch of stringy bark. He bites off a piece to chew and offers me the rest. *"Mangez,"* he says, urging me to do likewise. As I hesitate to bite down without first wiping the dirt off the root, he throws back his head and laughs at my squeamishness. It tastes of licorice, and he explains that I'm chewing on absinthe, an underground root with shoots that protrude from the soil every few feet. He tells me it's used to flavor pastis, the popular Provençal cocktail I sampled earlier in the week.

On our drive home from the Camargue, I reflect on the week spent with the Mures. What comes to mind has nothing to do with the monuments, museums, or art galleries we've visited. Instead, I envision Colette bouncing around the kitchen in her jumpsuit pajamas, midi meals on the terrace, a blazing Camargue sunset sinking below a fringe of wind-whipped marsh grass, and leisurely strolls through Paul's garden.

Colette interrupts my reveries to point out three cypress trees staggered in size that stand like sentries behind a farmhouse gate. "They are the Provençal sign of welcome. One offers food and lodging, the other protection, and the third, friendship," she explains, squeezing my hand. I can't think of a better way to describe the rewards of my belated sojourn as a junior abroad.

Lynne Vance is a freelance writer and public relations consultant who resides with her husband in Silver Spring, Maryland. During a twenty-year writing and editing career, her work has appeared in The Washington Post, The Philadelphia Inquirer, *and the member newspapers of Maturity News Service. Apart from travel, Lynne is addicted to swimming, chocolate, and used book sales.*

⋆ ⋆ ⋆

God as *Pâtissier*

*Metaphysical lessons emerge from
a hunt for culinary miracles.*

I HAVE A PALM-SIZED ICON THAT I FOUND ONE EASTER ON CORFU
in the shop of an impulsive, affectionate woman named Mrs. Gift-of-
God. The painting shows three angels dressed in ruby-colored caftans,
sitting together at a round table covered with a beautiful sea-green
tablecloth, just the color of the Aegean in certain lights and depths.
You can tell they have come a long way; they have the slightly weary,
relaxed posture of people who have arrived at their destination after
a long flight, and their bare feet are propped on soft cushions. They
look cheerfully hungry; on the table are three tiny forks and three
golden goblets, the same gold as their wings and halos. They are talking together with delicacy and wit, judging from the inclinations of
their heads and the appreciative smile of the angel on the right. It is
obvious that the cool wine in their glowing goblets and the aromatic scent of their dinner cooling is inspiring them. I know they
represent the angels who visited Abraham in the desert and that,
theologically, they are supposed to prefigure the Holy Trinity, but I
don't care. For me they are the angels of the table, presiding over
one of the arts of peace, the arts in which the sensual and the spiritual, the physical and metaphysical love, are fused into one substance,
far more difficult to accomplish than any of the arts of war.

My gastronomic guardians, who traveled with me throughout Greece, are the patron saints of the answered prayer, which every good meal is, and they remind me of one of the most important elements of Greek cooking. If French cooking is an ongoing inquiry into the ultimate rules of cuisine and Italian cooking explores the nature of impulse and improvisation, Greek cuisine, with its combination of frugality and richness and its transformation of scarcity into plenty, is a demonstration of the miraculous. Think of the olive, a bony-looking tree with a fruit no bigger than a fingertip, which can be turned into pies, sauces, fuel, and even light itself.

In Greece, when you go to the herb and spice seller for a handful of bay leaves, what you ask for is Daphne, the name of the nymph who gave this flavor to the world, the legacy of her flight from Apollo and her transformation into the laurel tree. Greek life is thoroughly entangled with myth, but nowhere more intimately than in the kitchen, where someone wielding a wooden spoon is always sure to remind you that the Greeks like to say that their words for cooking and magic are related. And one of the most charming double entendres I know I learned when I was searching for a rolling pin, called a *plastis*, which is another name for the Creator of the Universe. I was delighted to think of God as a breadmaker, perhaps even a *pâtissier*—at last we had something in common.

Greek cooks are past masters of the loaves-and-fishes method of cooking, feeding a full table of hungry guests and children with expandable handfuls of beans or a scant pound of meat that turns into a voluptuous moussaka or a *pastitsio*. But the dishes that seem closest to the Greek ideal of food, appearing in different combinations through each season, are the *yemista*, stuffed vegetables with different fillings. These demonstrate the two principles of the best Greek cooking: the love of freshness and the appetite for the miraculous. The *yemista* are edible treasure chests, *trompe l'oeil* main courses. Probably the most famous are stuffed grape leaves (*dolmathes*), but in the fall there are golden quinces stuffed with lamb and pine nuts (*kydonia yemista*), food out of fairy tales, and eggplant stuffed with rice and quail (*melitsanes yemistes me ortykia*), for which the island of Mytilini, otherwise known as Lesbos, is famous. In the winter, there are onions encasing rice, meat, and currants (*kremidia yemista*), and in Macedonia, *yiaprakia* for Christmas dinner (pickled cabbage leaves surrounding pork and dill). In spring, there are artichokes heaped with meat and cheese (*anginares yemistes me kraes kai tyri*) and delicate leaves of romaine enfolding rice and scallions and served with egg and lemon sauce (*maroulo dolmathes*). But my private passion is for zucchini blossoms filled with rice or bulgur, either gently sautéed or simmered in white wine and herbs. They have a flavor as indescribably rare as truffles and a texture that combines the melting with the crackling, like good kisses, a dish as erotic as summer itself.

Last July, over dinner with a friend at one of my favorite restaurants in Greece, Prinkiponisia of Thessaloniki, which specializes in the food of Greek Constantinople, I begged for advice about where to spend August 15th, the great feast of the Greek summer, celebrating the Dormition of the Virgin Mary.

"Every place celebrates a little differently," my friend said. "Do you know what you want?" I jumbled together pilgrimages, beautiful beaches, miraculous icons. "Miracles?" he said, "You want miracles? You want zucchini flowers. Where you want to go is Mytilini. In my home village there, we have a miraculous icon; we make the best ouzo in all of Greece at the distilleries in Plomari; and as for food, the Virgin Mary herself got hungry on Mytilini. One August when she was passing through and the heat was getting to her, she regained her appetite and her health eating our August mackerel and grapes. This is a fact everyone from the island knows."

So, later in August, a month known in some parts of Greece as the Banquet Bringer, I took the ferry to Mytilini.

I went first to Vatera, a village on the southern coast of the island, bound for the Vatera Beach Hotel, a place with a promising reputation for good food, which boded well for people in search of zucchini flowers. I drove down the main road toward the southern peninsula, through caramel-colored mountains and stunning pine forests.

Vatera turned out to be utterly refreshing; the hotel overlooked a crescent of sandy beach and a clear, jewel-colored sea, ample for contemplative walks at sunset. Every day you would see the guests waiting to read through the new lunch and dinner menus before their first swims, as if they were anticipating a new chapter in an irresistible serial novel. There were thrillingly fresh grape leaves, the best *tzatziki* I tasted in the country, stuffed eggplant that had the sweetness and fleshiness of a peach, rabbit *stifado*. The seasoning—herbs from just outside the back door—was an elegant heightening, like slightly darker pencil strokes defining a sketch's outlines. It was the food of artists—but there were no zucchini flowers.

On the day of the feast of the Dormition of the Virgin, the mountain village of Ayiasos, with its miraculous icon, was crowded with pilgrims. It smelled richly of pine and lamb roasting on the spit. I saw a boy with a shaved head, an earring, and a leather jacket stamped with the image of a skull and crossbones carrying a large candle into church to light before the icon of the Virgin Mary. I bought a homemade bottle of the most romantic liqueur I have ever encountered, with jasmine buds floating in it. But there were no zucchini flowers.

I gave up expecting them; like so many of the best Greek dishes, they were probably the privilege of home kitchens. I went to Petra to see its famous church, madly placed on a jagged cliff—Our Lady of Vertigo—and to the stately fortress town of Molyvos, with its castle overlooking the sea. From there, I had a personal pilgrimage to make to Skala Sikamia, a little fishing village where the novelist Stratis Myrivilis had written a dreamlike novel about Mytilini called *The Mermaid Madonna*, in which he describes an icon of the Virgin portrayed as a mermaid. I had been told he had written it in a tiny chapel overlooking the sea, where the icon itself was preserved. Skala Sikamia was miniature and perfect: a square shaded with plane trees and grape vines and smelling of honeysuckle, a pride of brilliantly colored fishing boats, and a chapel seemingly set in the sea itself, more like a caïque than a chapel.

I went right away to the little chapel of the Mermaid Madonna; a family was inside, peering intently into the bare corners, fanned out to look for the image. But there was no mermaid.

Below the chapel I saw a woman sitting in the courtyard of her shop, reading a novel, and went to ask her about the icon. She smiled and said, "There is no icon." I was puzzled, because I had been shown a picture of it. "Yes," she said, "there are pictures, but the icon itself does not exist. There are pictures inspired by the novel, pictures of what Myrivilis dreamed, so you have learned in Skala Sikamia the difference between Greek art and the art you know in the West. In the West you paint reality in all its details; in Greece we struggle to paint what doesn't exist."

Metaphysical lessons are best followed by lunch. I sat under the trees at a taverna called the Cuckoo's Nest and drank a flowery white wine, looking across at the coast of Turkey. The waiter said that they were making zucchini flowers in the kitchen. I asked if I could watch, and followed him to a corner where a woman was sitting with two chairs in front of her, one holding a wooden trough of zucchini flowers, the other a bowl of filling, one I hadn't encountered before, of feta and egg seasoned with shreds of fresh mint.

"They should be picked the same morning you are going to serve them," said the cook, "and if possible, before the sun comes up, when their throats are more open. You can see how delicate they are," she said, and handed me a weightless blossom and a teaspoon of filling. Coaxing the filling into the flower was like feeding a hummingbird with an eyedropper.

"Some people dip them into fritter batter," she said. "I don't. You'll taste why." I thanked her and went back to the table under the sweet shade. The first plate of zucchini flowers came out, with another carafe of white wine—elusive, dreamlike blossoms transforming a fleeting August afternoon into the unspoken goal of every traveler, an immortal day.

Patricia Storace, a native of Mobile, Alabama, was educated at Columbia University and the University of Cambridge. She is the author of Dinner with Persephone: Travels in Greece, *from which this piece was excerpted. Her essays have appeared frequently in the* New York Review of Books *and in* Condé Nast Traveler.

Chocolate with Julia

A portrait of a "foodie" is drawn
by many mentors.

SOMETIMES I FEEL LIKE I'M PART OF THE LAST GENERATION OF women who learned to cook from their mothers. Now, don't get me wrong, Ma was not a stay-at-home, all sweetness and light Betty Crocker clone. She worked day and night at a loud, scary sewing machine, making luxurious slipcovers for furniture owned by people who lived in the suburbs. We lived in a cold-water flat in central Newark, New Jersey.

Today I am a restaurant columnist for a major newspaper and write restaurant guidebooks. Before that, I had my own catering company, and I have cooked professionally in restaurants. If I had to trace how I got here, I would think it all goes back to three women in my life, but especially my mother.

I think my mother had about thirty recipes, all of which were in her head. And although she was French Canadian by birth, her food repertoire included the recipes from her Jewish, Italian, and German friends. I grew strong and tall on her stuffed cabbage, beef hash, spaghetti sauce, and spinach kugel.

I can remember visiting her friend Anne Franchino when I was about four or five years old. I was just tall enough for my nose to rest on the kitchen table. I watched amazed as Anne eventually transformed a mound of flour with an egg broken in the middle into gossamer light ravioli.

My first cooking experience came around the same time, when my mother walked me through a recipe for pineapple upside down cake. We placed canned rings of pineapple and brown sugar and butter in the bottom of the pan. Then we made the batter and plopped it on top, smoothing it gently.

Later, when we turned it onto a plate after it was baked, all I could do was stare in wonderment at the glazed pineapple on top and the brown sugar-butter sliding down the sides—my first creation. That night, my Uncle Lou, a Hemingway-type guy and my favorite uncle, stopped by and ate a piece of my cake. I remember all the praise I got for my "first" cake. Is it any wonder I've been seducing men with my cooking just about all my life?

But two women, whom I would meet later in life, had almost as much impact on me as my mother. It all came about when I returned from Manhattan in the '60s, after a life of free love, herb smoking, fun, and debauchery. I moved back in with Ma and together we started the second half of our life together—cooking.

At that time, our local public broadcasting station was showing both the original *French Chef* series with Julia Child and a series of Chinese cooking shows hosted by restaurateur Joyce Chen.

In no time, I had schlepped a wok back from New York's Chinatown and Ma and I were exploring Chen's cookbook. One night *egg foo yung*, another *moo goo gai pan*. Ma shopped for the food and did some of the chopping. I came home and wailed on the wok.

Stir-fries weren't our only endeavor. When Joyce Chen sealed every orifice of a duck, and then slipped the nose of a bicycle pump in between the skin and flesh and pumped the little bird up—I did too. After all, Peking duck was worth the effort. When one of my uncles saw the puffed up duck on a hanger over the sink, while a blowing fan aided in drying the skin, he wryly remarked to my mother, "I always knew that kid was a little off." But when the Peking duck was roasted and Ma and I were eating the glass-like crispy skin on our own homemade buns with hoisin sauce and scallions, we had the last laugh on him.

After awhile Ma rebelled against all that veggie chopping and I started to get soy sauce fatigue. So we began to follow Julia Child and her adventures in classical French cuisine. I bought her book, better knives, and some heavy-bottomed pans. I followed her recipes to the letter. Well, almost.

Six times I tried to make mayonnaise by slowly adding oil drop by drop to a beaten egg. Unfortunately, I curdled the emulsion several times with my hasty pouring. In a way, mayonnaise taught me patience, and I built up the muscle in my forearm.

After a particularly good meal one Christmas, I overheard my mother bragging about the duck à l'orange I had prepared. We had taken a Polaroid of the dish, which she showed to the neighbors. I think they mostly thought we were either off the deep end or uppity.

Years passed, Ma had died, and I had become a real foodie, writing for a local food-oriented magazine. A call came in one day, asking if someone at our hippy-dippy magazine would like to interview Julia Child.

Needless to say, I was first in line. For two weeks before the big day, I asked everyone I knew, "If you could ask Julia Child one question, what would it be?" The day of the interview, I took a cab to the Ritz-Carlton. Of course, I asked the cabbie the same fateful question. He said, "Ask her how she doesn't get fat on all that cream and butter she eats." Secretly I would have loved to ask her that question, but thought I might get clobbered for being so probing and personal.

Dressed conservatively in my one suit, I waited in the lobby, nervously checking my little Sony tape recorder, while all the while pacing the marbled hallway. Finally they came and got me and led me to the private elevator that went to the club floor lounge.

On the way up, I asked the white-gloved operator my Julia Child question. He began to mumble something as the door opened to a lounge full of people reading papers and sipping coffee, poured from silver pots. I waited in the lounge and then was summoned to Julia's suite. Entering, I was shocked at how bare it looked with a settee, coffee table, and my heroine herself, Julia. Even though I am tall, she towered above me.

She invited me to sit on the settee. With knees knocking together, I perched precariously, laid down my tape recorder on the coffee table, and took out my notebook and pen. I began to introduce myself and, with voice cracking with emotion, I told her how my mother and I had explored French cuisine with her book and TV shows.

Julia smiled, but quickly moved to change the subject. I thought for a split second that she was afraid I would ooze off the settee like a badly made *crème brûlée*. My first question was, "What is your advice to young chefs today?" She dug into my question, because she had just returned from France, dining around Paris with her friend Patricia Wells, the writer.

"Young chefs need to make food that people can actually eat easily, not have to deconstruct. I find all this mile-high food too architectonic—too many fingers on the food," she said with passion.

As she talked, I felt like one of those plate jugglers at the circus, since I was trying to make eye contact, watch that the tape recorder was moving, and take notes all at the same time. I was wrapped as tight as a stuffed pork loin.

Julia must have sensed my discomfort, because she kept smiling at me and talking softly. All of a sudden I looked at her well-lined face and saw the light emanating from it, and thought this is gonna be O.K., it's all gonna be fine.

Next, I asked her what advice she had for young homemakers.

One day listening to the radio, I was surprised and impressed to hear Julia Child discuss her early career in the intelligence world. A conscientious and career-minded young woman, Child worked for the OSS in its early days. Alas, the job was short-lived. "I was not well-suited to the spy life," she said, her famous vibrato resonating from the radio. "I'm quite tall, you know—I wasn't very good at *lurking*."

                    —Kathy Meengs,
                    "Julia's First Job"

With equal forcefulness she said, "Dine together. Families must eat together—it's so important."

Chiming in on what I thought was her train of thought, I said, "And all that fast food—it's a disgrace."

The words were no sooner out of my mouth than she said, "I love McDonald's, when you're traveling from Cambridge to Vermont, they'll kill you at those roadside truck stops."

Knowing I had made a major faux pas, I backtracked as fast as I could, stammering something about their healthy grilled chicken sandwiches.

Without any hesitation, she said, "I love a Big Mac with everything on it."

We talked some more and then it was time to go. She led me to the door and on a nearby antique table, a triangular piece of mirror was covered with about fifty Godiva chocolates. As we passed the table, she asked, "Would you like a chocolate?"

I felt odd having a chocolate at 11 A.M., as if I were chugging a martini at an early hour, but how could I turn down an offering of food from my guru?

I selected a chocolate, and shortly afterward I was out in the hallway, shakily making my way to the private elevator. As I walked down the hallway, I held the chocolate in front of me like a beacon and I thought, "I will never, ever eat this chocolate from Julia." Just then I looked at my hand and noticed that the chocolate was melting all over my fingers. With great pleasure and complete abandon, I popped the luscious morsel into my mouth.

GraceAnn Walden is the restaurant columnist for the San Francisco Chronicle. *She also leads culinary-history tours of North Beach, the traditional Italian neighborhood of San Francisco. She lives on Telegraph Hill with her dog Shibui and cat Kinky.*

Dishes for Collectors

The day that justice wasn't done.

A DISH OF PORK AND PRUNES SEEMS A STRANGE ONE TO CHASE TWO hundred miles across France, and indeed it was its very oddity that sent me in search of it. The combination of meat with fruit is not only an uncommon one in France, it is one which the French are fond of citing as an example of the barbaric eating habits of other nations, the Germans and the Americans in particular. So to find such a dish in Tours, the very heart of sane and sober French cookery, is surprising, even given the fact that the local prunes are so renowned.

I knew where we would go to look for the dish because I had seen it on the menu of the Rôtisserie Tourangelle on a previous occasion, when there were so many other interesting specialities that it just hadn't been possible to get round to the *quasi de porc aux pruneaux*. But this time I hoped perhaps to find out how the dish was cooked as well as in what manner such a combination had become acceptable to conservative French palates.

Driving out of Orléans toward Tours, I observed for the first time the ominous entry in the new *Guide Michelin* concerning the Rôtisserie Tourangelle: "*Déménagement prévu*" it said. Very well, we would get to Tours early, we would enquire upon entering the town

whether by some ill-chance the restaurant was at this moment in
the throes of house-moving. If so, we would not stay in Tours, but
console ourselves by driving on to Langeais, where there was a
hotel whose cooking was said to be worth the journey. The evening
was to be our last before driving north towards Boulogne, so we
especially didn't want to make a hash of it. But we had plenty of
time, the afternoon was fine, the Loire countryside lay before us in
all its shining early summer beauty. We dawdled along, making a
detour to Chenonceaux on the way.

So in the end it was after seven o'clock by the time we had bat-
tled into the main street of Tours, found the Office of the Syndicat
d'Initiative, and made our enquiry. No, said the pretty and efficient
young lady in charge, the house-moving of the Rôtisserie
Tourangelle had not yet started. All was well. "*Déménagement prévu*,
indeed," said my companion, "what a fuss. It'll be *prévu* for the
next two years." Fifteen minutes later the car had been maneuvered
into the courtyard of the charming Hotel Central, we had booked
our room, the luggage was unloaded. As we were about to get into
the lift I returned to the desk and asked the lady in charge if she
would be so kind as to telephone *chez* Charvillat and book us a
table, for we were already late. As I walked away, I heard her saying
into the telephone "*Comment, vous etes férme?*"

Yes, the *déménagement* had started that day. Closed for a fortnight.
Well, it was hardly the fault of the charming girl at the Syndicat,
but…anyway, it was now too late to move on to Langeais. We must
eat at Tours and make the best of it. By the time I had explained
the magnitude of the disaster to Madame at the desk, she and I were
both nearly in tears. For she perfectly grasped the situation, and did
not think it all odd that we had driven two hundred miles simply
to eat at chez Charvillat. But all the restaurants in Tours, she said,
were good. We would eat well wherever we went. Yes, but would
we find that dish of *porc aux pruneaux* which by this time had
become an obsession? And in any case what restaurant could possibly be as nice, as charming, as comfortable, as altogether desirable
as that of M. Charvillat?

Madame spent the next twenty minutes telephoning round

Tours on our behalf, and eventually sent us, somewhat consoled, to a well-known restaurant only two minutes walk from the hotel. I wish I could end this story by saying that the place was a find, a dazzling revelation, a dozen times better than the one we had missed. But it was not as dramatic as that. It was indeed a very nice restaurant, the headwaiter was friendly, and we settled down to some entirely entrancing white Vouvray while they cooked our *aloes à l'oseille*—shad grilled and served with a sauce in the form of a runny sorrel purée. In this respect at least we had timed things properly, for the shad makes only a short seasonal appearance in the Loire. It was extremely good and nothing like as bony as shad is advertised to be. Then came this restaurant's version of the famous pork dish, which turned out to be made with little noisettes of meat in a very remarkable sauce and of course we immediately felt reproved for doubting for one moment that an intelligent French cook could make something splendid out of even such lumpish-sounding ingredients as pork and prunes.

It *was* worth all the fuss, even for the sauce alone. But, almost inevitably, it was something of an anticlimax. The combination of a long day's drive, the sampling during the day of the lovely, poetical wines of Pouilly and of Sancerre *sur place* (and whatever anyone may say, they *do* taste different on the spot), a hideously ill-advised cream cake at an Orléans patisserie, the alternating emotions of triumph and despair following so rapidly one upon the other, not to mention a very large helping of the shad and sorrel, had wrecked our appetites. By this time it was known throughout the restaurant that some English had arrived especially for the *porc aux pruneaux*. The helpings, consequently, were very large. By the time we had eaten through it and learned how it was cooked, we were near collapse, but the *maître d'hôtel* and the *patronne* were just warming up. If we were interested in local recipes, what about their *brochet au beurre blanc* and their *poulet à l'estragon*, and their *dodine de canard*? To be sure, we should have had that duck as an hors d'oeuvre, but just a slice or two now, to taste, and then at least we would have some local cheeses and a sweet?

Curiosity overcame prudence. We did indeed try their *dodine de canard*, which was not the *daube* of duck in red wine usually associated with this name, but a very rich cold duck galantine, which would have been delicious as an hors d'oeuvre, but after all that pork.... Cravenly, we ordered coffee. No salad? No cheese? No dessert?

As we paid our bill, expressed our thanks, and left with the best grace we could muster, I was miserably aware that we had failed these kindly and hospitable people and left them with the feeling that we did not appreciate their food.

It was a long time before I had the courage to set to work on that recipe. When I did, and saw once more the row of little pork noisettes, the bronze and copper lights of the shining sauce, the orderly row of black, rich, wine-soaked prunes on the long white dish, I thought that indeed it had been worth the journey to learn how to make something as beautiful as that. One day, with a better appetite and more stamina, I will go back to that restaurant in Tours and make amends for the evening when justice to their cookery was not done.

Elizabeth David is the author of numerous books on food and cooking in-cluding French Provincial Cooking, Italian Food, South Wind through the Kitchen, *and* An Omelette and a Glass of Wine, *from which this piece was excerpted. Prior to her death in 1992, she was awarded the Order of the British Empire and elected a Fellow of the Royal Society of Literature.*

JANIS COOKE NEWMAN

A Culinary Tour through Chinatown

When in search of healing, start with food.

THE ELDERLY CHINESE GENTLEMAN PLACES THE TIPS OF HIS FINGERS on my forearm and I stick my tongue out at him. He leans forward and peers into my mouth, so close I worry my breath will steam his thick glasses. My three-year-old son Alex, fascinated by this display, opens his mouth, revealing the plum-flavored candies called Haw Flakes the man has slipped into his hand.

"You're too moist," the man tells me, "too wet inside."

He's right. For weeks I've been suffering from a sinus infection that has made me feel as if I were walking around with my head submerged in a giant aquarium.

The man rips a piece of loose-leaf paper out of a notebook and fills it with Chinese characters—a prescription for the precise blend of roots and herbs needed to balance the five elements (earth, water, fire, metal, and wood) in my body. I watch the list grow as my husband examines the ground deer antler that is supposed to increase virility, and Alex tries to eat the pieces of orange off the small red altar in the back of the shop.

We are in Tung Tai Ginseng Company in San Francisco's Chinatown, a small herb shop crowded with cardboard boxes and barrels just the right height for my son's small hands, and filled with ginseng roots shaped like little men, dried black mushrooms that resemble clods of dirt, and large flat pieces of white cuttlefish. My husband tries to show Alex a tray of tiny dried seahorses, but he cannot distract him from what appears to be a small dragon flattened and mounted on a stick.

My husband and I have walked past these shops that smell of earth and saltwater and ginger hundreds of times on our way to the R & G Lounge's salt-and-pepper shrimp, the Oriental Pearl's "house special" noodles. But until today, we've never come in; the locked glass cases of shark fins and pulverized rhino horn making us feel as if they were not only foreign, but also forbidden.

We have only come today because of my sinus infection and my husband's sudden interest in Chinese cooking. Lately, our kitchen has been filled with dangerous-looking cleavers, two-foot long chopsticks, and little bamboo steaming baskets that Alex likes to stack up into tall round towers. And of course, cookbooks. *One Thousand Chinese Recipes. A Wok for All Seasons. The Joy of Wokking.* I flip through them while my husband stir-fries pieces of duck in crackling hot oil, reading about the particularly Chinese connection between food and good fortune ("always serve a whole fish during New Year to ensure prosperity"), and food and good health ("after a woman has given birth, feed her a soup made from black-skinned chickens to restore vitality"). Even

For acute conditions such as sinus infections, the best treatment is with herbs, but chronic problems of dampness in the body can be treated through diet. Foods that dry dampness tend to be bitter and/or aromatic and include vinegar, ginger, rye, amaranth, adzuki beans, turnips, pumpkins, yams, and rice. A simple, bland diet is best, and everything should be cooked without spices if possible. Foods to avoid include dairy, eggs, soya, concentrated sweet foods, and anything raw.

—Paula Mc Cabe,
"Healing through Diet"

Chinese medicine, I read, relies on things that can be eaten for its remedies.

The gentleman with the thick glasses hands my prescription to the herbalist behind the counter and gives my son another small round packet of Haw Flakes. We watch as the herbalist finishes filling a prescription intended for two small boys. Things that look like chamomile flowers, pieces of bamboo, and eucalyptus leaves are weighed on a scale he balances on a forefinger, and then piled onto small squares of pink paper. At the very top of the pile, he places several large dried insects.

"What are those?" my husband asks the boys' father.

"They live in the trees…" the man says, trying to think of the word. He makes a clicking sound with his mouth.

"Cicadas?" I say.

"Yes, yes, cicadas," he nods.

I am enormously relieved when nothing I can recognize as a bug is added to my pile of roots and herbs.

The herbalist totals my bill using an abacus—$15 for the herbs, $10 for the doctor—and gives Alex yet another packet of Haw Flakes.

We walk out into the bustle of Grant Avenue. Chinese matrons in polyester pantsuits push past us like small forces of nature, their shopping bags filled with thin white rice noodles, red bottles of chili oil.

At the Sun Tong Lee produce market, baby bok choy and long thin purple eggplant overflow the rough wooden bins. I watch a woman poke at the same winter melon for what must be ten minutes, weighing it in her hands and pressing her nose up against its fuzzy skin. Beside her, a much younger woman with a baby bound to her back holds a bunch of long beans up to the sunlight, assessing their deep green color.

I remember reading that "the same balance the Chinese herbalist works to achieve in the body, the Chinese cook works to achieve on the plate." So, crunchy water chestnuts are covered with a silky sauce made from smoked oysters. Sweet braised pork is served alongside salt-baked squid. In light of this philosophy, the woman with the fuzzy melon is no less of an alchemist than the doctor who examined my tongue.

Alex runs down a narrow alley, stopping to listen at a half-opened basement window where we can hear the clicking of mah-jongg tiles. Deep in another alley we come to a tiny poultry shop. The sign above the door reads "Never Ending Quail." Here, behind glass walls covered with advertisements proclaiming that food stamps cannot be used for live birds, we see cages filled with chickens, squab, partridges with bright red and blue feathers; but oddly, no quail. Alex hangs on the counter, his eyes wide, as a chubby woman in a padded silk jacket is handed a brown paper bag that is making a clucking sound.

My husband studies the birds, who appear jumpy, and decides that he is not yet prepared to personally wring the neck of our dinner. Instead, we walk over to the Dragon Market where fresh fish glisten on ice, and even fresher fish swim around in big tanks.

A tiny Chinese woman with white hair pulls up the sleeve of her sweater and reaches a thin brown arm into one of the tanks, grabbing a silver-scaled sea bass on the first try. She hands it to a man in a white apron who knocks it on the head with the back of his cleaver. Alex is standing on his toes so he doesn't miss anything as the man guts the still flapping fish, and I'm not certain if I am a bad mother for letting him watch, or a good mother for giving him this unique cultural experience.

My husband shouts out for a couple of live Dungeness crabs, and they are pulled from the water by a man who is fearless about sticking his hand into a tank filled with serrated claws. While we wait for our crabs to be weighed, Alex points to an armadillo I hope is dead, curled up on the scale.

"Is that for you?" an old Chinese man in a San Francisco Giants baseball cap asks us.

"Oh no, no," my husband says shaking his head. The armadillo is put in a plastic bag and handed to an Asian woman in a business suit. She holds the plastic bag with the armadillo in the same hand as her leather briefcase.

"I'm hungry," Alex says, and although I have not quite gotten over the hard-bodied creature in the plastic bag, we go to Lichee Garden for a dim sum lunch.

The restaurant is crowded and noisy, the sing-song of Cantonese blending with the staccato of English and the clatter of metal steamers hitting the tables. Alex feasts on *har gow*, steamed dumplings filled with sweet shrimp, without offering us any, and I realize that dim sum is perfect kid food—lots of small portions you don't have to wait for. Each time a waiter presents us with a tray, we take something—steamed Chinese broccoli, bright green and tasting of oyster sauce; *sui mai,* ground pork and shrimp tucked into a yellow noodle shaped like a flower; transparent wheat starch dumplings filled with hot scallions and earthy mushrooms. When he's had enough, Alex plays under the table with a little girl wearing a backpack covered with Japanese cartoon characters, while my husband and I finish off the last of the shrimp and leek dumplings washed down with cold Tsingtao beer.

After lunch, we walk along Stockton Street, the crabs making scuttling sounds in their paper bag. Alex wanders into Chinese grocery stores where plastic-wrapped loaves of Wonder Bread sit next to packages of dried salted jellyfish. To the Western nose, the smell of a Chinese grocery store is totally foreign—a blend of fish, sweet dried fruit, and soap powder.

The sinus infection makes the front of my face feel heavy and watery, and I want something hot to drink. We push Alex's stroller up Broadway, where buses completely painted over with advertisements for the latest summer movie are grinding their way up the hill, to the Imperial Tea Court.

Inside, it is lovely and quiet—antique mahogany tables and chairs, Chinese silks on the walls, a long dark wood counter behind which glass canisters of rare teas are displayed. A group of local men sitting at a big round table in the back have brought their songbirds. Carved wooden cages hang from the scrollwork overhead, and tiny yellow and red birds flutter their wings and chirp as we order our tea.

At Alex's insistence, my husband chooses Monkey Picked Tikuanyin, which we are enormously disappointed to learn is no longer picked by monkeys. I choose Jasmine Pearl. The tea master sets a small kettle on the hot plate on our table and presents the tea leaves to us, holding a small porcelain dish under our noses. The Monkey Picked Tikuanyin smells like toasted almonds, and the Jasmine Pearl, which is indeed shaped like tiny seed pearls, smells like fresh tuberose.

While the tiny caged birds sing above our heads, I sample my husband's tea, which tastes fermented and sweet, and sip my Jasmine Pearl, which is perfumey and pleasantly bitter. Alex eats an entire bowl of sweet cookies and salty crackers.

When we get home, my husband boils the crabs in a broth made from ginger and scallions and we eat them with Sichuan green beans that are so spicy hot they make the insides of my ears itch. Afterward, I empty my pink packet of roots and herbs into a pot of water and boil them for an hour. The house smells exactly like the Tung Tai Ginseng Company. After I strain out the leaves and pieces of stick, I'm left with a thick brown tea that has a sweet licorice taste and coats my tongue, making me gag. I have to hold my breath to drink it, and within minutes I feel hot and flushed and want to go to bed.

That night, I sleep deeply and have no dreams that I can remember. The next morning when I awake, the aquarium feeling has completely disappeared.

Janis Cooke Newman is a writer who lives in Northern California with her husband and son Alex. She is the author of The Russian Word for Snow: A True Story of Adoption.

Easter Nachos in Warsaw

An invitation to a party calls for
some cultural creativity.

I HAD SPENT THE PAST TWO DAYS SEARCHING WARSAW FOR CHEDDAR cheese. "Use Mimolet," my veteran expat friends told me. "It's the same color, and no one will be able to taste the difference." But I had tried Mimolet, and I guess my taste buds are simply more refined than those of my friends, or simply not as accommodating. I was planning a dinner party, and my recipe for Tex-Mex chicken enchiladas called for cheddar cheese. And I wasn't willing to settle for anything besides the real thing.

I started at the Polna Street Market. It's a well-known fact among expat circles that this is the place to go for those hard to find, must-have American items. It had taken me a while to locate it, well hidden in a less-traveled part of town, but at Polna Street Market I had found Nestle's semisweet chocolate chips. I had bought Philadelphia cream cheese. And I had found fresh raspberries in January. Surely they would have cheddar cheese. Kraft even.

Wrong. Not a single stall-keeper had heard of it. "What is this, '*ser* chedDAR'?" they would ask, translating "cheese" to *"ser"* and placing the emphasis on cheddar's last syllable. I tried to explain, to no avail.

I tried the French and Danish hypermarkets on the outskirts of

Warsaw. They had amazing selections of cheese. Large wheels of brie and Camembert. "How about Emmentaler?" one surprisingly helpful deli clerk suggested, in English. But no *ser* cheddar.

I tried a small Polish grocery store, knowing full well they wouldn't have it either. Tired and annoyed, I finally went into the Texaco Star Market. Admittedly, this is where I buy most of my groceries. It's on the corner of my street, and it is a small but well-stocked store offering groceries but no gas. Never before had they had cheddar, but today, the day before Easter, the store packed with people, I found *"Ser Chestar"* in the deli section. *Chestar?* I thought to myself, as I read the hand-written label poked into the block of cheese. It *looks* like white cheddar. *Could it be?* I looked closer. I nearly squealed in delight. In small, red letters on the yellow wrapper, I read, "Cheddar Cheese, made in Wisconsin."

I bought a whole kilogram. That's 2.2 pounds of cheese. I didn't care. I was celebrating victory.

I came home, my arms laden with bags to drag up to my apartment. The flyer taped to the door of my building meant nothing to me except for the words *"Wigilia"* (vigil), the date, time,

Agnieska is neat in appearance; her secondhand sweatshirt, jeans, and sneakers hint at her meager income, yet she continues to splurge on anything edible at the kiosks and street vendors along the way. She grasps my backpack in one arm, juggling it along with plastic bags of miniature cucumbers in fresh pickling brine, loaves of rye bread wrapped in brown paper, herbed farmer's cheese, and packets of mixed chocolates. Soon, my one free arm is filled too—with fresh cheese, potato *peirogies*, *jagoda* berry jam—the other arm still clings to hers. Our cornucopia of goodies makes it impossible to thumb through our Polish-English dictionaries, so we barely speak. Her guiding eyes and hands pull me in the right direction; my smile indicates my contentment, as we communicate without words.

—Renee Restivo, "Dinner by the Baltic Sea"

and the name of my apartment complex. I deduced that there must be some sort of Easter recognition, today, Saturday, the vigil of Easter. And apparently, as a resident of the complex, I was invited.

I called Tee, my American neighbor and reliable source for all things complex-related. "Hi. It's Kristi," I said into my cordless phone, and we chatted while I put away my groceries. Then on to business: "Listen, Tee...is there some party tonight?"

I had called it—Easter Vigil, in the courtyard. And yes, of course I was expected to be there. "Everyone comes, brings the kids. We don't understand any of it either...just smile and nod," she said.

"I assume there will be vodka, like Christmas?" My stomach churned in remembrance. We had stood outside in the courtyard, the men having raised a thirty-foot tree, freshly cut and dragged from the forest. They were cold, and vodka was the remedy.

"I wouldn't think so," Tee replied, "with Lent and all."

"Maybe they break the Lenten fast when the sun goes down." Somehow I couldn't imagine any Polish festivity without vodka. I made a mental note to eat a carbo-laden late lunch.

"Oh," Tee said, as if she could read my thoughts, "You have to bring something to eat."

My mind raced. "Any ideas?" I asked, surveying my empty refrigerator, which I was loading with supplies for my dinner the following night. Unfortunately, I hadn't bought much in my two-day scouring of Polish grocery stores.

"They always want me to bring deviled eggs, but I hate making deviled eggs," she said.

"A lot of trouble," I agreed.

"Some sort of finger food. See you around 7:00."

Some sort of finger food? It was 3:00, I was meeting a friend for coffee, and I had to come up with an hors d'oeuvre before 7:00? *Nachos.* I heard a voice. It continued, *Easy. Finger food. You even have a KILO of cheddar. It's divine providence.*

I argued with the voice, *But no one will eat it.* Generally speaking, Poles are averse to anything remotely non-bland.

At 6:45 I slid the pan of nachos into the oven. It was a strange conglomeration of Pace Picante sauce and sliced green chilies from the Embassy commissary, with a local brand of tortilla chip and my hard-won cheddar cheese.

Ten minutes later the doorbell rang. Tee and Tom, with their beautifully presented plate of deviled eggs. I pulled the pan out of the oven with my Texas flag potholders. "NACHOS????!!!" they exclaimed together. They were looking at me, wanting some sort of explanation for my nonsensical idea. "I know, I know," I told them. "No one will eat them, but I *had* to bring something, and this is all I could come up with." Tee was laughing so hard at me, she was almost crying.

"At least I'm not going empty-handed. Right?"

We headed downstairs. In the center of the courtyard, a table had been set with five plates of deviled eggs, several plates of finger sandwiches, and cracker rounds with anchovies and herring. My neighbors eyed my pan suspiciously as I approached, but Margareta graciously made room on the vinyl tablecloth for whatever it was that I was carrying.

Silently, everyone formed a circle and Jan, the apartment super-intendent, picked up one of the plates of eggs and presented them one by one to each neighbor. *Oh God,* I thought to myself, *He's going to serve everyone from each plate and they're all going to think they have to eat one of the nachos.* I looked at Tee in horror. She simply shrugged, suppressing a giggle.

Each person took an egg and held it, waiting for everyone to be served. When the circle was finally complete, everyone bowed their heads. *Ah, a prayer,* I thought, as Jan began to speak. I followed suit, looking down at my egg. A few moments later, everyone looked up as if on cue and ate their egg. *Surely they won't complete this communion service with vodka,* I thought to myself.

And just as I was thinking this very thought, shot glasses were passed and the bottles were opened.

The fast was broken, the solemnities ended. The circle broke up, people mingled and laughed, and continued to eye the pan of nachos. It remained untouched. But I wasn't too disheartened, as no one seemed to be much interested in the solid refreshments.

Marcin came over. I was relieved to have someone to talk to in

English, but I was also counting on him to give me a hard time about the nachos. "What *is* that anyway?" he asked, his head indicating the general direction of the offensive platter.

"Nachos. From Texas," I explained, as if that made them somehow acceptable.

"O.K. No one will like them, but they want to know how to eat them."

I laughed. No wonder the strange looks. They were looking at a pan of melted cheese with red and green stuff and they had no idea how to try it, *if,* of course, they were so inclined.

So I led Marcin and his father Jan to the table to demonstrate. People stayed in their little groupings, but conversation stopped and I sensed all eyes on me.

The stage was mine. "See," I said, "You grab a little corner of chip and pull…"

I heard a communal "ahh" of understanding. My moment as Houdini. "And then you eat it." Marcin followed suit, reluctantly, and then, even more reluctantly, admitted that it wasn't *too* bad. We drifted back over to Tee and Tom, when Jim, the other American in the complex, arrived with a surreptitious bottle of wine.

I looked back at the table and everyone was crowding around. Moments later, my pan was empty.

And there were still four plates of deviled eggs, and the finger sandwiches and herring remained untouched.

"They like it!" Tee and I exclaimed, astounded and proud of our victory for Texas, fought so far from home. I felt a tug on my sweater. It was Adam, the precocious seven-year-old who lives two floors above me.

"Kristi," he asked, "What you call this?"

"Nachos." I told him. Fascinated with English, Adam always greets me with the stilted dialogue he learned at school. Now we were getting somewhere, I thought.

He ran over to his mother and her small crowd, and then ran back to me, and very slowly enunciated each word, "How you make this, machos?" *Ah…nachos become machos in Polish.* I laughed to myself.

In simplified English, I carefully explained how to make them, leaving out the green chilies and substituting a local brand of very bland salsa. Adam hung on to every word and then raced back to the group, speaking animatedly in Polish.

And then he came back one last time, "My mother says, where you buy this, '*ser* chedDAR'?"

After teaching for the past five years at the American Schools of Warsaw and El Salvador, Kristin M. Roberts has left teaching—at least temporarily—to pursue travel writing and photography full time. With rapid capitalization and Westernization in Poland, cheddar cheese is now widely available in Warsaw.

* * *

Please Pass the
Snails, Mom

A sophisticated palate isn't only for adults.

WE HAD READ THAT WELL-GROOMED LAP DOGS ARE WELCOME AT most restaurants in France. What we did not know as we embarked upon our two-month European vacation was how these same establishments would respond to our eight- and six-year-old children, Molly and Gus, whose table manners, I'll admit, we've often compared to those of the friendly beasts.

French restaurant pups sit patiently at their masters' feet, hoping always for the well-seasoned handout, presenting no more of a nuisance to restaurant staff and guests than, say, a large handbag. Children can be altogether different—especially ours, who are inured to threats, distinctly self-possessed, and incapable of maneuvering a stemmed water goblet from table to mouth and back again.

So it was with a certain amount of apprehension one rainy midday that we abandoned plans for a picnic and opted instead for lunch at Les Pyrénées in the little Basque village of St.-Jean-Pied-de-Port, one of those *bien connu* restaurants around which a real gourmet would plan an entire vacation.

An experienced mother had once advised me to dress the children well if they were going to dine in public. Well-dressed children tend to be well-behaved children, and even if they aren't they still look cute. Heeding her advice, I dug deep into the duffel bags until I found the matching blue belts that looked so natty with the children's plaid Bermuda shorts. It was the best I could come up with on a cold rainy day in the Pyrenees.

"How many stars?" Molly asked upon entering the restaurant, as if keeping stats for the season. It's amazing how quickly they caught on to the Michelin mantra of touring: "How many stars?"

As soon as we'd settled into our velvet high-back chairs, the waiter, perhaps familiar with the danger posed by idle children, set about pleasing his young clientele. But instead of the usual crayons and paper placemats, here the children were presented with a tiered platter of delicate *amuse-bouche*, literally "mouth entertainment." They were amused; who wouldn't be with morsels of bass from the nearby mountain brook and miniature *salmon en croûte*. It was in fact the perfect solution, in that a full mouth is usually a silent mouth.

I felt even more at ease when a French family with four small children was ushered to the table next to ours. These children appeared even more rain-sodden that our own. Moreover, they were not wearing belts. Nobody seemed to mind. Dining in France is far more basic than dress.

Our waiter proposed an elaborate menu for me and my husband; for the children, ours as well as our neighbors', a sure-fire lunch of steak and French fries, or, as the children quickly learned to demand, *"frites."* Along with all the *feuilletés, terrines,* and *charlottes,* our chef seemed equally skilled at serving up (for a modest price!) half a dozen miniature steaks and, how can I describe them, perfect French fries. You'd have thought he got his start at an upscale grade-school cafeteria.

Encouraged by what turned out to be a memorable lunch, we began reading our red Michelin Guide with new zeal. For most of our stay in France we had rented furnished apartments, which meant we could eat at home. We therefore determined that occasions when we did eat out should be special. We evolved a workable routine whereby Molly and Gus would order their meals—they were fast becoming junior connoisseurs of French fries—while my husband and I settled back for the standard two-hour French repast.

Our children were warmly welcomed at every restaurant we visited. Indeed, the stereotypical image of the snooty French restaurant has more to do with dining in New York than in the French countryside or even in Paris.

Many restaurants offered reasonably priced children's meals. Otherwise, chefs willingly prepared simple dishes not listed on the menu—sometimes omelets or chicken but usually a steak with *frites*. Moreover, they invariably showered the children with all sorts of little extras: *amuse-bouche*, home-baked breads, intricately crafted tiny pastries.

After finishing their meals the kids liked to slip outside to play. We tried to choose restaurants next to parks or in traffic-free parts of town. My husband and I could enjoy lunch in relative tranquility until dessert time when the children, without fail, would reappear with hungry looks on their faces, eager to consume the better half of my *ile flottante, gâteau au chocolat*, or *crème brûlée*. And thus we journeyed through France, saving francs, sharing calories, and exposing our children, if not to French cuisine, at least to French fries.

I was, in fact, secretly grateful that our children could be bought off so inexpensively. While dining in the Norman seaside town of Honfleur, we were seated next to a French family with two boys just about our children's ages. Their boys, however, were not interested in the *frites*. After a lengthy discourse with the proprietress on the quality of the *foie gras* versus the smoked salmon, they opted for an order of each. Meanwhile, Molly and Gus, still babes in the woods when it came to gastronomic sophistication, were perfectly happy with their *omelets au nature.*

With time, however, our children inevitably became intrigued by the various dishes that preceded their parents' desserts. We encouraged them to remain at the table and, like good parents, offered bites of different delicacies. This may have been a mistake, for even the most timid eater seated for long hours in a French country restaurant will eventually find the tastes, the texture, and the flavors irresistible. Molly and Gus soon developed a modified poodle pose, their mouths moist and slightly open, their eyes riveted to our forks.

In Caen, we chose to eat at another well-known restaurant, La Bourride, famous for its Norman cooking and conveniently situated in a traffic-free zone. Perfect for the kids, we thought. But after a remarkable *amuse-bouche* of mussels and celery, the children sensed a good thing. They were determined this time to sit it out.

Somewhere amid the procession of courses, I was served a plate of six oysters cooked with apples and Calvados. I offered one to Gus, ate one myself, and noted his wistful gaze.

"I'm sorry, Mom, but that's just so good." I sheepishly helped myself to another and passed him the remaining three.

I love my son, I shared all of my meal, even the green apple and Calvados sorbet between courses, even—to my amazement—the *tripe á la mode de Caen*. What mother could deny food to her hungry child? And as Gus worked his way through my *tarte Normande* in its sinful puddle of *crème anglaise,* I consoled myself by calculating all the calories I was being spared.

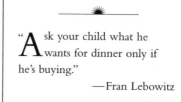

"Ask your child what he wants for dinner only if he's buying."
—Fran Lebowitz

By the time we reached Paris, the children's palates were becoming a bit too refined for our budget. On the eve of our departure from France, we dined at an over-priced yet festive Alsatian restaurant in Les Halles. Molly, who by this time was understandably pleased with the bits of French she had picked up, ordered her favorite cocktail: L'Exotique, a lovely rainbow striation of fruit juices that cost ten dollars. Meanwhile, Gus, who cannot read English or French, passed his menu back to the waiter.

"I'll just have snails and a salad," he said.

Snails and a salad: that came to thirty-five dollars for his "light" supper. I politely told the waiter that we needed more time and then proceeded to explain to Gus that snails were a specialty of Burgundy. Here in Paris he should really try the (moderately priced) onion soup. It worked and I breathed a sigh of relief knowing that long before Gus learned to order *foie gras,* we'd be high over the Atlantic, fast on our way to the land of hamburgers and catsup.

Libby Lubin travels frequently to Europe—often with her husband and two offspring, all of whom understand and appreciate the art of good eating.

LAURIE COLWIN

English Food

*Who says the English don't
have decent food?*

IF YOU WORK UP THE COURAGE TO CONFESS THAT YOU LIKE ENGLISH food, people are apt to sneer and tell you that it is impossible to get a decent meal in the British Isles and that the English know nothing about cooking. Even the English, some of whom have been brought up on a dread substance known as School Food, often feel this way.

England, of course, has a long and grand tradition of cooking— it is a much plainer and more forthright variety than that of France and, since it is of a cold climate, it does not have the sun-drenched style of, say, Italian food, but it has pleasures all its own.

The first time I went to England I was a student and virtually penniless. I can't remember what I ate except a plate of custard at a cafe near Victoria Station and a gooseberry bread pudding in Canterbury. A slightly richer friend took me out for tea one afternoon at a place called Heals in the Tottenham Court Road.

Heals, in the early sixties, was a cross between Hammacher Schlemmer, Design Research, and the present-day Conran's. It sold top-of-the-line pots and pans and fixtures. Young marrieds furnished their households at Heals, where you could get linens, lamps, knives, forks, plates, and so on. On the top was a tea room, which has since vanished.

We sat down to tea and I was in heaven. This was the wish fulfillment of a childhood filled with English children's books. It seemed a wonderful feast to me as a child and now that I am grown up, tea is my favorite meal. But until I sat down at Heals I had never had a proper tea in my life. All around us were real Englishwomen—there did not seem to be a man in the place—pouring out tea from brown teapots. Put before us was a plate of bread and butter, a seed cake, and a dish of little cakes made with candied cherries. I felt I would never be as happy again as I was that afternoon.

On my next trip I stayed with my friend Richard Davies and his parents. At the Davieses' I was introduced to the institution of English Sunday lunch: roast meat, potatoes, two vegetables, and a sweet. I learned that even when the papers bore the banner headline: WHEW! WHAT A SCORCHER! the meal never varied. You might sit around the swimming pool at someone's country house and still emerge to be fed roast leg of lamb, roast potatoes, two vegetables, and dessert.

It was on this second trip that I had my first cream tea, which many people feel is in itself the perfect meal: scones, clotted cream, and strawberry jam. As you drive out of London you begin to see signs on houses that read WE DO CREAM TEAS. My cream tea was consumed at a tea house in Woodstock, right near Blenheim Palace, on a day thick with clouds. The tea shop had one large room full of

---

I find that little of what I cook is based on my heritage. The lone exception to this is my great-grandmother's shortbread, which she brought with her from England to America. This recipe is the one thing that ties me to our collective past and may link us to our future, as I've passed down the recipe to my children. My hands work the buttery dough as she would have done and the rich smell permeates the kitchen. The taste of it with a cup of tea binds me, however slightly, to her and my cultural and familial history.

—Susan Brady,
"The Ties that Bind"

tables dressed in white clothes. We sat down and consumed an amazing quantity of scones, cream, and jam.

On my next trip I was more grown up, better heeled, and I decided it would be nice to do some cooking. I found myself wandering happily in the local shops and supermarkets where everything was so pleasingly different from what I saw at home. A trip to the Harrod's food hall filled me with awe. I have never seen anything to compare it with: the dozens of local cheeses and the variety of imported ones. The numbers of birds and kinds of eggs. The fish, pâtés, and cuts of meat I had never heard of.

In England you could get chicken that tasted like chicken, and gooseberries and tomatoes and those long pale green cucumbers with a silvery taste. In specialty shops there were raised pies: veal, ham and egg, chicken, and cottage pie. You could buy a bag of delicious cream cakes and eat them in the movies. You could even find a decent cup of coffee, although nothing compares to plain old English tea.

To divert me from my endless meanderings in food stores, Richard took me on a trip to the highlands of Scotland, where we were assured we would never find anything edible at all. On a freezing night in June we had dinner in our hotel and decided to order haggis, as a joke. Haggis is the national dish of Scotland. It is composed of minced liver and oatmeal (barley is a variation) in a savory sauce, stuck into a sheep's stomach and boiled. It is served with something called "mashed neeps," which are turnips. It sounded so dire that we felt we ought to try it.

The haggis was brought to our table in its stomach bag, which was slashed before our eyes. Out slid the contents, which gave off a very delicious smell. To our amazement, we loved it. It was rich, savory, just right for a cold place and perfect with the slightly bitter turnips.

While wandering around the highlands we ate magnificent smoked salmon, soused herring, wonderful bread, biscuits, and something called Scotch tablet, which is a solidified bar of butter and sugar.

It is possible to get nasty food everywhere, but with the exception of a few eccentric meals fed to me by my peers, the only awful thing I ever ate in England was a packaged pork pie; but then a person who eats a packaged pork pie gets what she deserves.

Once the English food addict is back on home turf it is possible to stave off pangs of longing with the aid of any number of English cookbooks from which you can make such wonderful things as Queen of Puddings, Easter biscuits, potted shrimp, ginger cake, lemon sponge, Bath buns, orange custard, Lancashire hot pot, and crumpets, which I have attempted many times, never with any success.

My copies of Jane Grigson's *English Food* and Mrs. Florence White's *Good Things in England* are falling apart. For late night reading I enjoy Mrs. Arthur Webb's *Farmhouse Cookery*, which has no copyright date but looks to have been published in the twenties and has descriptions of the Welsh Grate, the Devon Down Oven, the Suffolk frying pan, and contains recipes for things like Whit by Polony (a kind of sandwich filling of minced beef, ham, and bread crumbs) and Singing Hinnies (a griddle cake). I am also fond of Alison Utely's *Recipes from an Old Farm House*, which describes a pudding made from the milk of a newly calved cow should you happen to have one around the house.

One of my greatest finds, in an old bookshop in the Hamptons, is a copy of *From Caviar to Candy: Recipes for Small Households from All Parts of the World*, by Mrs. Phillip Martineau. First published in 1927, it covers the territory from hors d'oeuvres to sweets and poses such questions as: "Now, why, I ask, should the same old fare be invariably provided at cricket lunches? I remember a cricket lunch at Hurlingham Club in the Argentine…" Her first chapter, entitled "Cooks—Mistresses and Imaginations," sets the tone: "What chance has the average cook, unless her mistress will help her?" she asks. This is a question I have asked myself many times.

Her recipes are more chatty than scientific—"There be some that claim that it is worthwhile even to visit that dullest of all dull places, Bagnoles-de-l'Orne, to eat the tripe prepared at a nearby town," begins one.

When it comes to cakes and puddings, savories, bread, and tea cakes, the English cannot be surpassed. If you love English food there are many things you can make at home and you can find things at specialty stores. But the one thing you can never find, which lovers of English food dream about at night, is double cream.

When the English come to the United States and see what we call cream, they cannot believe their eyes. What we call heavy cream they get for free on the top of their unhomogenized milk, which is delivered in glass bottles by actual milkmen.

When Americans see what the English call cream, they cannot believe their eyes. My first encounter with double cream took place at my first encounter with English Sunday lunch at the Davieses' house in the country. We had just finished our roast beef and it was time for dessert. Out came a bowl of raspberries and a large gravy boat.

"What's in there?" I asked.

"Cream," they said.

I turned the gravy boat slantwise but nothing poured out. I felt this might be some sort of joke since all eyes were on me. I gave the gravy boat a little shake but nothing emerged.

"Try a spoon," said Richard's mother.

I did, and what I scooped out was the consistency of cold molasses or very thick homemade mayonnaise. I plopped it onto my berries.

"This is *cream*?" I gasped.

"Double cream," they said.

Since it was the most delicious thing I had ever eaten, I went on a kind of binge of double cream, which, it seemed miraculous to me, you could simply go into a grocery store and buy. I especially liked it slathered on little pancakes that came six to a package. McVittie's Scotch Pancakes have now disappeared off the face of the earth.

Back in the States, so great was my longing for double cream that when Richard, who lived in New York, went home for Christmas, I asked him if he would bring me a pint.

I met him at the airport one cold January night. He emerged from customs, tall and rattled-looking, carrying a dripping bag out in front of him as if it were a wet fish. His coat sleeve and his shoes were covered in double cream. The lid had slipped off in the bag, the container had slipped sideways, and the resulting mess caused considerable interest among the Customs inspectors.

"What is that?" said the Customs man to Richard.

"It's cream, for a friend," Richard said. The Customs man gave him a hard look, and then his face softened. He spoke gently, as if to an insane person.

"We have dairy products in the United States, too, Mr. Davies," he said.

But anyone who has been to England could have told him that we don't have cream.

Laurie Colwin is the author of numerous novels and short-story collections. She is a Guggenheim Fellow and the recipient of a grant from the National Foundation for the Endowment of the Arts. This story was excerpted from her book, Home Cooking: A Writer in the Kitchen.

PART THREE

THE ADVENTURE OF DINING

STEPHANIE ELIZONDO GRIEST

A Culinary Revolution

So much for being a vegetarian.

DINING AT A POPULAR BEIJING RESTAURANT CALLED YU ZUI (FISH Lips) convinced me there was no limit to what my Chinese pals would eat. Just about anything that could fly, swim, crawl, or slither could be slathered in batter, deep-fried, and served on a stick. Grasshoppers. Larvae. Beetles. Scorpions. Duck fetuses. I once saw a six-year-old schoolgirl with pigtails sucking on the tentacle of a shish-kebabbed octopus like it was a lollipop.

This was hard to handle. Growing up in Corpus Christi, Texas, celery salt was the most exotic spice in our cupboard. Mom told Dad on their wedding night that she'd cook once a year and we learned to relish the lasagna we got each Christmas. I was raised on the pot pies Dad heated up for lunch and the dish of the day at whatever diner he drove me to for dinner. I ate roast beef and tater tots at Furr's Cafeteria on Mondays, chicken fingers with fries at Andy's Country Kitchen on Tuesdays, fish sticks and hush puppies at Catfish Charlie's on Wednesdays. Waitresses not only knew my name, but my latest grades and the most recent score of my team's Little Miss Kickball game as well. I was, in short, my father's meat-and-potato protégé.

An environmental kick refined my taste buds in high school.

Joining Greenpeace turned me off veal; I shunned frog legs after leading a student protest against dissection. By college, I was a full-fledged, militant vegetarian living in a seventeen-member housing cooperative with such a strictly enforced meatless policy that we once denounced someone for sneaking in a box of Kentucky Fried Chicken. Our shelves were lined with herbs and spices I'd never even heard of, like turmeric, cardamom, and cumin, and my house-mates whipped up weird things like moussaka and ratatouille. After three years of this cuisine, I assumed my taste buds had reached their highest evolved state. I was mistaken.

My culinary revolution had only begun.

Soon after college I moved to the People's Republic of China to work at the English-language newspaper *China Daily*. My first afternoon in Beijing, the executive editor held a banquet in my honor. I knew it would be a meal like no other when he told the secretary we would return in two and a half hours. A haze of cigarette smoke and chili vapor enveloped me like a veil as we walked through the front door of a crowded restaurant down the street from our office. It was noisier than a high school cafeteria, but the mainly male clientele paused mid-chopstick to gawk at me—the *laowai* (foreigner)—as we squeezed past. Few wore shirts and there wasn't a hairy chest among them.

> Vegetarians always say, "I never eat flesh" in a way that puts you right off your nice little beefsteak.
>
> —Agatha Christie,
> *Agatha Christie A to Z*

A team of waitresses ushered us into a separate banquet room filled with plastic plants and equipped with a karaoke machine. All fourteen of my colleagues and I easily fit around an enormous round table. The executive editor immediately demanded the menu, which turned out to be the size of my hometown telephone directory. As he flipped through it, everyone started shouting out orders that our waitresses frantically recorded onto thick pads of paper. Ordering seemed almost competitive: if someone made a poor selection, the others uttered a guffaw. A good choice, however, won hushed whispers of approval. Food is the ultimate fashion to the Chinese. No one of status would be caught dead eating last year's dish.

The editor glanced my way and asked if there was something in particular I wanted to try. Fearing I would offend my carnivorous colleagues, I diplomatically replied in Lonely Planet Mandarin that I liked to *chi dofu*, eat tofu. That response brought gales of giggles around the table; the editor turned bright red. I couldn't imagine what was so funny—unless I had mispronounced *dofu*. Tones are sacrosanct in Chinese: *Ma*, for instance, can mean horse, hemp, or mother depending on the intonation. *Zhi* can be toilet paper or vagina. Later that week, however, I happened to notice a sexy lass saunter past a pack of Chinese bachelors. As soon as she was out of earshot, they started whispering about wanting her *dofu*. I never asked for it again.

From there, my colleagues began preparing for the upcoming meal. First they dumped hot tea over their saucer-sized plates to sterilize them and tossed the liquid onto the floor. Then they unsheathed their chopsticks from paper wrappers and rubbed them together with concentrated care, like butchers sharpening their knives. I was trying to pry my wooden chopsticks apart when the door opened and a waitress lugged in a giant trash bag that appeared to have something alive thrashing about inside. I peered in and found a gargantuan, gasping fish. My heart went out to it.

"*Hao ma?*" the waitress asked.

Using chopsticks is an art—with many rules of etiquette:

- Do not lick or chew on your chopsticks;
- Never set your chopsticks down parallel across your rice bowl (bad luck);
- Do not stab your chopsticks into your food so that they stand straight up in a vertical position (reminiscent of a common funeral ritual);
- Never point or gesture with your chopsticks (impolite).

—LB

I gulped and nodded that yes, in fact, this soon-to-be-battered fish was quite *hao*, good. The woman bowed, slung the sack over her shoulder and disappeared as another waitress entered with the first course of cold dishes and plunked them atop the spinning Lazy Susan in the center of the table. Then she darted out of the way as the chopsticks started flying. It seemed an almost Darwinian pursuit for the tastiest morsels—and only the aggressive survived. Fat and bones were spit upon the table with vigor. Soups were slurped. Burps resounded with gusto. I cautiously dug my chopsticks into the nearest sampling without a face—a translucent something decorated with red and green flecks—and gulped it down.

"You like pig?" the colleague beside me, Xiao Ma, asked. His name means Little Horse, but I preferred calling him—in English— My Little Pony.

"That was pig?"

He smiled and tapped his elbow to signify which piece of pig I had just eaten. I smiled meekly by way of reply. Being a closet vegetarian was going to be tougher than expected. Next, I took a scoop from a bowl of bright yellow jiggly somethings that smelled faintly of chicken noodle soup but appeared meatless nonetheless. The fatty jiggles left a greasy smear as they slid across my plate, but the long, slim, solid thing in their midst was vaguely appetizing. I picked it out with my chopsticks, popped it in, and twirled it around in my mouth. Suddenly, it pierced my inner cheek. I spit it onto my plate and gawked in amazement. After years of eating chicken fingers at diners across America, I had finally been served a real one. Claw included.

My stomach started growling as I gazed longingly at the rest of the dishes atop that Lazy Susan. There was an entire roasted duck, sweet and sour spareribs, stewed pork belly with veggies, squid with green peppers. The fish that had been flopping only twenty minutes before had been steamed and served head to fin on a bed of what looked like grass. It all smelled heavenly, but there wasn't a thing my vegetarian self could eat.

"Don't you like Chinese food?" my editor's voice suddenly boomed from across the table.

Every last colleague turned to face me. I panicked. "Oh no! I mean, yes! Yes, of course!" For reasons that elude me, something Julia Child once said popped into my mind. "I could happily eat Chinese food every night for the rest of my life!"

My decision became all too clear. I could either offend a table full of colleagues by sticking to my college principles or I could sample a 3,000-year-old cuisine that boasts some 5,000 dishes. Can't morals be shoved aside for a little culture now and then? I'd only be in China once—how many other times in my life could I try barbecued bear paw? I kissed off my vegetarian inclinations and added my chopsticks to the frenzy. I gobbled up prawns smothered with garlic, which—admittedly—were rather scrumptious. The chicken served Sichuan style with whole red chilies and peanuts was downright delicious. Taiwanese dried beef tickled my taste buds; the sea slugs made them sing. Initially I munched for culture, but before long, I was crunching for pleasure. Oysters and black bean sauce. Fish ball soup with white radishes. The succulent tastes converged in a party on my palate; a taste bud had an orgasm. Julia Child was really on to something here!

My year in China culminated as it commenced, with a two and a half hour banquet. This sumptuous meal started off with a live snake and turtle, which were brought to our table for the ceremonial nod of approval. The snake, upwards of three feet in length, thrashed madly about in the waitress's hand, but the turtle stayed tucked inside its shell. We protested. The waitress smiled triumphantly, removed a hairpin, and jabbed it up the turtle's rump. Its arms, legs, and head shot out.

"*Hao, hao,*" we murmured and dismissed her with a wave. I tried to picture how the cooks would prepare the turtle and decided they would shish kebab its little stumps. Mmmmm.

The waitress returned about ten minutes later with a silver platter full of shot glasses filled with a dark red liquid. Chinese liqueur was usually red, so I didn't think much of it until we did a toast and I raised a glass to my lips. Then it occurred to me the liquid did not look too smooth. In fact, it was borderline chunky.

"Zhe shi shenme?" I whispered to my colleague Mao Lan, Mountain Wind. "What is this?"

"Snake blood," she said matter-of-factly and gulped down her glass.

I closed my eyes and shuddered. Granted, I had eaten a lot of crazy things that year in China, but there was no way I could ever go back to vegetarianism if I drank the freshly-squeezed essence of life. Greenpeace would revoke my membership. The People for the Ethical Treatment of Animals would put me on their hit list. This was worse than eating veal.

I had worked up to that moment the past twelve months. I took a deep breath, tilted my head back, and chugged the blood. It burned like vodka and left a trail of residue. Before I realized it, a burp escaped. A primal one, with an aftertaste. My Chinese colleagues looked at me in surprise. Smiles crept across their faces as I unsheathed my chopsticks and gave them a good rub.

"Hao chi," I replied nonchalantly. Tasty.

Stephanie Elizondo Griest has written for The Washington Post, Latina Magazine, The New York Times, *the* Associated Press, *and Travelers' Tales. When she isn't wandering the world, writing about popular culture or rambling about food, she is belly dancing and working on an online history project for kids, The* Odyssey: U.S. Trek. *This story is excerpted from her completed manuscript,* Seeing Red: Tales From the Communist Bloc.

JULIE JINDAL

Hungarian Rhapsody

You'll eat it, or else.

JEAN AND I TRUDGED ALONG THE DARK, WET SIDEWALK, WONDERING if we'd missed the restaurant, or if it had closed down. We squinted at corner street signs and building numbers. "This place had better be good," I said as it started to rain. Jean quickened her pace, and I hurried to keep up with my friend's long-legged stride.

We were in Vancouver, British Columbia, on business, and she'd heard of an authentic Hungarian restaurant near the waterfront. I imagined pasty goulash, gray mystery meat, and sauces choked with paprika, but I didn't want to disappoint her by seeming too conservative.

This was not my first culinary adventure with Jean. We had traveled through China together, devouring everything under the sun. We had also popped dozens of antacid tablets. Pork dumplings in Xian produced one particularly memorable night hunched over the toilet. But now we were in Canada, the epitome of safety and civility. I told myself—with the slightest swagger—I could take anything this city dishes out.

Nestled between off-ramps and dead-end streets, with a cluttered view of shipyard booms, a tiny whitewashed house emerged from the damp mist. Compared to nearby high-rises, the cottage looked like a mushroom among redwoods. A hand-painted "open" sign beckoned. I followed Jean through an arched wooden gate and bounded up the steps. A few yellowed, framed restaurant reviews hung on the cramped vestibule's walls, but we didn't stop to read them.

A man in his mid-fifties sat at a desk near the entrance, slouched over a battered hardcover book. He wore dark pants, a white shirt, and a vividly embroidered blue and red vest, which I imagined was Hungarian. He looked up when we said hello.

"Do you want to eat?" he asked, his pale blue eyes measuring us from under his wispy eyebrows and wire-framed glasses. He didn't ask "How many?" or "Smoking or non?" His only question was whether we wanted food.

When we said yes, he stood up, straightened his shoulders, and led us to a table for two near the front window. His slight pot belly was supported by a small white apron tied around his hips. He gave us menus and vanished into the kitchen.

Jean and I noticed that we were the only patrons, though it was just past 7:30 on a Friday night. The dining room was long and narrow. Brightly colored crockery and linens adorned the clean white walls. A large, slightly disturbing oil painting depicted rural women with vacant bovine eyes. I shuddered and concentrated on the canned folk music emanating from the ceiling.

The menu looked intriguing, with Hungarian names and English descriptions in an ancient typeface. There was plenty of meat, as I expected, which suited me but wouldn't have pleased my vegetarian husband. As a faint aroma of hot oil wafted from the distant, silent kitchen, I settled in to select a meaty indulgence.

Our maitre d' reappeared—apparently he would be our waiter, too. Jean told him we were new to Hungarian food. What would be a good introduction?

He sighed heavily. "What a problem. What a terrible problem," he repeated over and over.

He asked what we knew about Hungarian food. I confessed my ignorance, though Jean piped up and asked if they used a lot of chili. She meant chili powder similar to paprika, but a vision of Texas chili must have sprung into his mind, and he recoiled as if she had burned him.

"No! Chili is very bad! A Hungarian restaurant serving chili would not be Hungarian! How could you ask that? Never, never eat chili!" Even after she explained herself, our host still huffed and paced with displeasure.

He launched into a story about a culinary competition. The finalists were Hungary, England, and the United States. The Hungarians made a wonderful dish. But they lost! The English placed second with fish and chips, and the Americans won with a hot dog. He banged his palm on a nearby table, rattling the silverware. "Can you believe it? A lousy hot dog could beat the finest Hungarian dish?" Unsure whether to believe him, we cooed our sympathies.

He leaned against another table, crossed his arms, and declared an introduction couldn't be done. We would have to jump in.

Bravely, Jean asked for the sour cherry soup. Perhaps still stinging from her chili question, he gruffly asked her if she knew the soup was chilled and very sweet. She said that it would be all right and his eyes narrowed. Then she ordered the trout.

"That's the least Hungarian

When I was a child, an endearing elderly Hungarian woman named Ida used to care for my siblings and me. I'd come home from elementary school and open the door to be greeted by Ida and the warmth of the kitchen, where I knew she spent most of the day. The hearty potato goulash—my favorite—was a recipe she brought with her from the old country. As a child, I'd stand on a chair by the stove and watch her magically finish preparing the dish. I never wrote anything down and when Ida passed away, her goulash recipe went with her. I've been trying to re-create Ida's nourishing goulash, but I've never been able to do it. Something is always missing. I don't thing it's the amount of paprika I'm using— I believe it's the love she used to add when I wasn't looking.

—Lisa Bach, "A Taste of Childhood"

thing on the menu," he muttered. She started to change her mind
and he interrupted her. "It's the best trout you will ever eat. In
Hungary, it's the only fish we make." How could she argue with
him? She asked for *langos* (fried bread) and he grunted approval.

I pointed to the lamb chops, asking if they were good. He practically flew into the rafters again. "Of course they're good!
Everything here is good!"

"But are they a good way to try something Hungarian?" I
quickly amended.

Edging closer, a little placated, he assured me they were quite
Hungarian. He shot another disapproving look at Jean. I said I
wasn't sure which soup I wanted, and he quickly solved that for me.
"You want today's soup," he announced.

"What is today's soup?" I asked, handing him my menu.

"It's the best soup you will ever eat." He turned and strode back
to the kitchen.

Jean and I looked at each other, eyebrows raised. The deserted
restaurant, the dark windows, all alone with a touchy Hungarian—
anything could happen. A band of Gypsies could magically emerge
from the bathroom, twirling like ghosts. Horsemen shouting com-
mands in Magyar could charge from the kitchen, their dark steeds
wheeling in a spangle of color. The doors and windows could
sprout bolts and noisily lock us in the restaurant forever.

Our host returned, walking through the echoing dining room,
and asked us where we were from. "Seattle," I said, and Jean mentioned Los Angeles. He wasn't sure where Los Angeles was.
However, he knew Seattle, and described an American customs
official searching his car at the Canada-United States border.

"I kept asking that obnoxious man, 'What are you looking for?
Maybe I can help you find it. I know this car quite well.'" He set a
hand on his hip and confided, "I'm not afraid of authority. Police
and officials don't bother me. Still, that man searched and searched.

"Finally I told him, 'I have little money, but I will not spend it
in your country with this sort of treatment.' So I left and went back
to Canada, and I haven't gone to America since." He strutted back
to the kitchen.

Jean leaned toward me. "I'm so sorry I suggested this place!" she whispered.

"No, it's all right," I whispered back. "We wanted to try something different, and this certainly fits the bill. You can apologize if the food stinks, how about that?"

Our host reappeared with two large, oblong pieces of fried bread, and our moods lightened. He placed a small glass dish filled with minced garlic between Jean and me, and advised us to ladle on plenty of garlic and salt. "Be sure to eat while it's hot," he said.

Escaping steam scorched my fingers as I tore off a puffy piece. The combination of garlic, salt, and hot bread eased my anxiety. The soup arrived during my second mouthful, and I incoherently mumbled my appreciation. Jean simply nodded, her mouth also full.

Having finished the fast-cooling *langos,* I turned my attention to the nameless soup. A shallow bowl held small flour dumplings, French-cut string beans and carrots in a clear, pungent broth, with herbs and spices floating on top. A thin band of paprika rimmed the bowl's edge, like ocean foam after a receding wave. With the first few spoonfuls, I understood how food critics could describe a dish as "assertive." Decoying me with an initial impression of dill, the soup's paprika aftertaste snuck up quietly and then leapt onto center stage, loud and boisterous. Entertained, I happily finished my bowl.

Jean's soup was more like a dessert. Tart cherries hid in the creamy pink sauce. After she found all the cherries, she sighed. "This is way too sweet," she said.

I peered across the table into her half-empty bowl. "You don't have to finish it."

"What? And admit he was right? I'm not giving him the satisfaction." She gripped her spoon tighter.

Our entrees arrived, and the fragrant, soothing aromas began to convince me that our host was merely an interesting character, not someone afflicted with a personality disorder. Yet I felt compelled to finish every bite or risk his wrath. My first bite boded well for cleaning my plate—the tender lamb fell apart in my mouth before I could chew it.

The best way to describe Hungarian food is to compare it to

music. My lamb chops proudly trumpeted their complex blend of flavors with strength and determination, like a high school band's Sousa march. They were tasty and they knew it. Jean let me sample her trout, which was more subtle. It reminded me of soft classical music played by a flute quartet, smooth and elegant.

Toward the end of my meal, though my stomach was about to burst, I was tempted to pick up my lamb bones and chew off the last flavorful shreds of meat. When our host came to collect our plates, I asked him if it's O.K. in Hungary to chew on the bones.

"What is rude," he said, "is to leave the bones. You should eat them."

I chuckled and looked up. The skin around his eyes hardened—he meant it.

He took my plate. "We do. We eat the bones. It's not hard, you break them open and eat them. In Hungary you eat everything." He sniffed and turned back to the kitchen.

Jean shrugged. "You should have tried it," she said, though her smile gave her away. We paid—the first time I ever tipped generously out of fear—and waddled toward the door.

"I'm glad you two girls came tonight," our host announced to our backs. "Otherwise I would have closed early and killed myself."

We brushed off his parting remark, certain he was joking. Yet as I lay awake that night, my stomach packed as tight and heavy as a medicine ball, his comment didn't seem so unlikely.

I rose from my lumpy hotel mattress and rummaged through my bags. "Jean," I asked, "did you bring any antacids?"

Julie Jindal is a freelance writer whose work has appeared in Seattle Weekly, ByLine Magazine, *and* Seattle Sidewalk.com. *She lives in Bellevue, Washington.*

PAM PEETERS

Of Cabbages and Kings of Beasts

A simple meal feeds more than the belly.

FOR ONCE WE ABANDONED OUR TRAVEL SCHEDULE. INSTEAD OF sticking to our plan of just a day trip, my husband and I decided to spend the night camping in the heights of the Aberdares, a national forest in Kenya, because we hadn't expected the minor mountain range to be so botanically interesting and diverse. At 10,000 feet, the night would be cold and damp and uncomfortable, but the great thickets of dense bamboo forest, vast stands of a giant tree-like heather, plus the potential of spotting the beautiful and rare Bongo antelope made us want to stay despite the sacrifice our stomachs would have to make for the extra day of fun. Our plan was to reward ourselves for the day of privation (nothing but bread, beans, and bananas) by rising early the next morning, driving to the nearest luxury lodge, and splurging on a gargantuan multicourse lunch. Had it not rained all night, it would have been a workable plan.

The trees were still dripping when we awoke. A black Serval cat tiptoed through the grass clumps by our camping van, oblivious to our presence inside, shaking diamond-bright drops of water off its head. Such sights remind us why, by preference, we camp. The comfort of the lodges, the obsequious servants, and the paved garden paths are all unnatural barriers we try to avoid—no matter how much, at times, we feel the need to seek them out. We crave the lodges because they are clean, civilized, and predictable. Camping never is, which is why it provides the best stories to mail home and the most chances to learn what a place is really like.

The Aberdares, we soon learned, is a place where, after a rain, it is too slippery to drive a VW van up a short but steeply-inclined campground access road. Our van was trapped, and we were all alone, nearly out of food, and cold, unable to build a fire with damp wood.

Walking, or even leaving one's car, is forbidden in Kenya's national parks. And with good reason. Tourists do, on occasion, get killed when they leave the safety of their vehicle. ("But he was only trying to feed the elephant a biscuit!") However, we were biologists. We knew caution and understood the potential dangers. The nearest ranger station was only seven miles away, and we were thrilled to have an excuse—even a flimsy one—to hike. We packed two bananas and headed out.

Hiking the flat main road was fairly easy at first, and we found ourselves dawdling over red wild gladiolas and brilliant sunbirds. The tracks in the mud were fascinating because they revealed how many animals lived in this magical, high altitude place.

A mile or so before the ranger station, the road turned uphill, and our pleasant hike turned arduous. On the mud-slick road, each uphill step defied gravity, and our feet slipped out from under us. We were grateful for the rhino footprints that made little level footholds for us, though startled that these hairless beasts would live in such alpine surroundings.

There were also the cloven dents of buffalo hooves, and finally came the lion paw prints. One really large cat and two smaller ones had very recently walked the road before us. Hmm. *How ironic,* I thought, *that in search of a meal, we might ourselves become one.* The round impressions gave our feet a decided fleetness; suddenly the slipperiness of the road no longer impeded us. We clapped and shouted at each blind curve (especially after the tracks disappeared into the giant tussock grass by the roadside), but, to our knowledge, all we ultimately surprised were the rangers.

Contrary to our expectations, the two uniformed guards manning the two little wooden huts were quite delighted to see us. Instead of berating us for stupidly risking our lives, they brought us chairs, hot tea, and a three-week-old newspaper. They radioed for a Land Rover to tow us out. We ate our bananas, watched a chameleon clamber amidst the pink flowers in the little garden of the station, took a walk with one of the rangers to look (unsuccessfully) for a Bongo, waited for the tow, and kept warm by a nice fire built just for us.

Still waiting hours later, our impatient stomachs growling, we were invited to join the rangers for lunch. We gratefully accepted and followed the men into the cooking hut, which was small, dark, smoky, and warm. We all sat on the floor around a large, bubbling pot as a steaming broth was ladled into dented metal plates. We were a curiosity to these men, who spoke little English and apparently had little enough contact with tourists to find us highly exotic and amusing. They watched us anxiously as we tasted their brew.

As my taste for Ghanaian food grew, my awareness increased as well. I learned that, unlike in the States, food left in a bowl was not thrown out; someone, maybe a child, would happily eat it after I had left. Unwanted table scraps were always recycled, fed to the family chickens or pig. Eventually I understood that rather than "cleaning my plate," I could in all politeness eat just a few bites of the food to acknowledge the host's hospitality and leave the rest for someone else.

—Kimberly Green,
"My Surreal Meals"

It was absolutely delicious. I smiled. *"Mzuri sana!"* Very good! The rangers beamed.

How different this whole scene was to one that had been etched in my memory just two weeks earlier in Paris, where I had sat, on a chair, at a table covered with a starched linen cloth, with a pretty little china bowl of soup before me, trying to catch the attention of the surly French waiter. That soup was memorable for all the wrong reasons: it was a lukewarm gray fluid tasting of dishwater—and thin, with a scattering of carrot shavings and a single cockroach for garnish.

By contrast, this wilderness soup was a masterpiece despite its humble ingredients; cabbage, potatoes, and onion browned in a generous amount of Kimbo brand lard all came together with wonderful layered harmony, a soup that not only tasted wonderful but restored the spirit.

Just as the right wine can make a meal, so can the proper meal complement a day. This was the perfect meal to cap off our adventure. I felt warm, happy, and full.

Pam Peeters combines good food and adventure as often as possible. She has volunteered as an art and biology teacher at her local school, written for her small town newspaper, and assisted her husband of thirty years in his careers as a zoology professor and wildlife artist. She lives in Sunol, California.

Funeral Feast

A local custom provides surprising nourishment.

I THOUGHT A FEAST INVOLVED EATING A LARGE AMOUNT OF FOOD with a large group of people, but I was wrong.

I had been hearing about the upcoming feast for months. It was to be an especially big feast, people said, a traditional funeral feast on the first anniversary of an important man's death. The year before, Uku'pata's husband, a "big man" in Su'u village, had died. His family would hold this funeral feast to honor him. This was also the traditional way to pay back the people who had helped during his illness.

This was not to be just a local event. People would be coming from "Town," town being Honiara, the capital city of the Solomon Islands. Honiara was on the same island as Su'u, and only about sixty to seventy miles away, but there were no roads and it was a crowded twelve-hour boat trip in the rickety Malatumey, a foul-smelling boat which had been discarded by the Leper Society of New Zealand. People also, we were told, would be coming from Malaita, the major island to the east.

I lived on Marau Sound at the southern tip of Guadalcanal Island, in an enclave of transplanted Malaitan 'Are'are people. The 'Are'are settled here about 150 years ago. The story is that when the

nine canoes of 'Are'are arrived in Marau there was no one living in
the area so they just moved in. I take the story with a grain of salt.
The 'Are'are are considered fierce by other islanders, and are feared.
The 'Are'are are the Mafia of the Solomons, and up to a couple of
generations ago they led a life that included hired killers and selling
out one's neighbor. Until the missionaries converted the island to
Christianity (at least in name), there was an unrelenting cycle of
revenge killing that explains the underlying uneasiness in the culture. The Birao (native Guadalcanalians) were a gentler sort, less
inclined toward warfare. Marau Sound is enclosed. It has calm
waters for the best fishing around, coral reefs for gathering shellfish
and easy spear fishing, and is a safe harbor. There is an area of rela-
tively flat land and small hills along the coastline for yam gardens
and coconut groves. I find it hard to believe that the Birao turned
their back on the Marau area, opting instead for the pounding surf,
harsh storms, and rugged terrain of the aptly named Weather Coast.

The week before the feast everyone in Su'u was busy. A twenty-
five-foot long "leaf" house was built out of palm fronds. It would
serve as kitchen, warehouse for all the food, and guest house for
those who would spend the night. Wood was chopped, coconuts
and kumara (sweet potato) collected. Several pigs that hadn't been
there before appeared in the village.

The day before the feast twenty pigs were killed and cooked in
Su'u. I avoided the village that day, but I wandered over in the
evening to see the preparations. Everything was under control.
Could I "kaikai pigpig?" the cooks asked. Yes, I could eat pig. So I
was given a "little bit" on a banana leaf to take home. My little bit
weighed about five pounds.

I was told so many times in the days before the feast that there
would be "plenty of custom things" to photograph that I got the
hint. No one would tell me directly, but I was expected to function
as feast photographer. This is not surprising, as I was the only one
in the area with a camera.

The 'Are'are are not known for directly sharing information. If
you ask questions people are happy to answer, but it doesn't occur
to them to tell you if you do not ask. If you don't know enough to

ask, you won't find out. And even when asked, the answers, from my American viewpoint, often seemed to circle about the issue, rather than coming to the point. Not knowing what else might be expected, I took a friend aside and asked what I should know. He told us that everyone, depending on the relationship to the family, would contribute pigs, kumara, bags of rice, maybe even custom money (strings of shell beads). Since I hadn't known the big man and wasn't around when he was sick, I could give ten dollars as my contribution. Good. I hoped that I had asked all the right questions and had gotten all the information I needed.

The morning of the feast I went to sit with the widow Uku'pata in the kitchen hut. Not much was going on. Her daughter Sivahui was sweeping the dirt floor. Rose was breast-feeding her son Joe (pronounced dji-oh). I was given some little bits of pork to eat. People would be coming soon, I was told. Soon, of course, was relative. A breeze rustled through the palm trees. We waited.

All family members bring with them large sacks of food and kava to be shared during the days of the funeral. They also bring woven tapa cloth, whales' teeth, and elaborately decorated mats. Some of these things will be buried with the body and the rest will be divided among everyone at the end. Kalisi tells me the funeral will last ten days. Ten days. The men are drinking kava, planning the arrangements. Up the hill, the women gather under large tents that seem to have appeared out of nowhere. They're chopping vegetables, pounding coconut into cream, cutting meat, preparing tonight's feast. I have a feeling the pig I've befriended in the crate box won't see this thing to the end.

—Laurie Gough, *Kite Strings of the Southern Cross*

At around noon the first group arrived from the village of Hatare. The women were carrying huge baskets of uncooked kumara on their backs, held on by a strap stuck to their foreheads.

They were also carrying cases of canned tuna on their heads! A roasted pig hung from a pole by its feet between two men. They went directly to the new leaf (palm frond) kitchen to deliver the food. Ninipua, Uku'pata's son, accepted the food. As at an American baby shower, who had brought what was carefully noted in a small book. More people arrived and soon there was a line of men with roasted pigs, and women with baskets of food outside the kitchen waiting to check in. Some groups had two or three pigs. A few people had shell money or cash. I joined the line and handed my ten dollars to Ninipua. It was duly marked in the notebook. A stream of people arrived throughout the day. By the end of the afternoon, in addition to the twenty pigs killed the day before, there were at least twenty-five more stacked in the new kitchen. The pile of kumara was attaining mountain status. There was carton upon carton of canned tuna. People just milled about, talking. The old women smoked their pipes, men chewed betel nut, and children ran in and out of the crowd. I took pictures. Kalisto, the area chief, a distinguished looking man with bright white hair and a long white beard, wore flip-flops, a lava lava (sarong), a faded "Life is Hell in the Tropics" t-shirt, and a string of human teeth made from his ancestors' conquests.

When the stream of arrivals ended, it was time to divide up the food. It was late afternoon. I was starting to get hungry. The village girls began making piles of kumara. There were three sizes of piles. Small for people like me who hadn't been involved when the big man died (I didn't even know his name), medium for most of the people there from the area, and large for those who had contributed most. After the kumara, the pork was divided, the big piles getting the heads and front-leg portions. Children were given the job of fanning with banana leaves to keep the flies at bay. The cartons of tuna were opened and added. There were, maybe, one hundred piles. Last of all, the shell money and cash were divided up between the largest piles.

Ninipua came out with the notebook. He and a man I did not know stood over one of the smaller piles of food. The man raised his hand and announced in a booming voice, "This portion belongs to George Otoia." The teenage girls delivered the pile to the recipient. He then would move on to the next pile. The process continued. "This food belongs to Dii-na" he called out, and I was brought a pile of twelve kumara, a back leg of pig-pig, a slab of fat, and two cans of tuna. There being so many piles, this process continued for quite some time. No one ate. It was evening. When the last and largest pile was announced (it went to the musicians who would play that night) everyone packed up the food they had been given and went home.

The feast was over. No eating had taken place. I took the pork, kumara, and tuna and went home to make dinner to share with the dog, Piglet, and Kusi, the cat. I was starving.

After eating kumara regularly for her two years in the Solomon Islands, Dana Squires only eats them now in the form of sweet potato pie at Thanksgiving. She has given up slabs of pork fat, but longs for the plant-ripened pineapples, the twenty-seven varieties of bananas, and the pink-fleshed papayas that grew right outside her door. She is an artist in Olympia, Washington.

KARI BODNARCHUK

✦ ✦ ✦

Hunger in the Himalayas

Food is a luxury item when money
is short and the hike long.

AFTER EIGHTEEN MONTHS ON THE ROAD, I HAD REACHED THAT burned-out, numb stage of traveling when nothing affects you, no matter how grand or intriguing. I realized this when I reached the Taj Mahal and my only reaction was, "Pretty. So where can I get lunch?" Before heading home, I decided to go trekking in Nepal, both to satisfy an old dream and to recapture the exhilaration I had felt earlier on the trip. I needed something to quash my growing indifference and only big landscapes have the power to really move me. Truthfully, I also wanted to arrive home trim and fit.

I am known, among my friends, for having a huge appetite. I can easily consume a foot-long sub, a quart of ice cream, and a batch of raw cookie dough without even loosening the belt buckle holding up my size eight jeans. It is easy enough to hike or bike away these calories at home, but this trip had offered more food temptations than workout opportunities. Still, after a year and a half spent mostly outdoors, I couldn't possibly step off the plane with a stomach pouch earned from eating Australian Tim Tams (a chocolate-covered, wafer-like cookie, so mouthwatering I couldn't eat fewer than six in one sitting), or wobbly thighs gained from sampling Asian treats and then sitting—immobile—on slow-moving buses for days on end, during which time the only real calorie-burning activity was walking ten feet to the toilets. Incidentally, those Asian treats included fried dough balls sold by the dozen at markets in Thailand; sweet Malaysian *martabak*, a dough square filled with chocolate (or bananas) and covered with heaps of mind-numbing, syrupy condensed sugar; and *mysorepak*, an Indian treat made from clarified butter, palm sugar, and flour. Of course, I closed my mouth a few times during the trip, to go scuba diving in the Andaman Sea, four-wheel-driving in Australia's dusty Outback, and hiking up sulfur-reeking volcanoes in Indonesia. And I really wasn't that soft or round, but as I said, I just wanted to be trim and fit. What I didn't plan on was trimming down to what I weighed at fifteen, half a lifetime ago.

To reach Nepal, I took a twenty-nine-hour bus journey from Varanasi, India (a trip that required six pieces of *mysorepak*, a loaf of bread, and a bag of cream crackers, and just two bathroom strolls). The bus dropped me in downtown Pokhara at the foot of Nepal's Annapurna mountain range. Here, I tracked down Rabindra, a friend of a friend, who lived near the Old Bazaar, in a small house with a big welcome mat. He was a kind man who turned his living room into cozy guest quarters for me.

Rabindra and I spent several days together, sharing stories and perspectives, and then he helped me plan a trek through the mountains. For hours, we hovered over maps, discussed options, and plotted routes. The proposed trek led from his doorstep in Pokhara to the Annapurna Base Camp (a 10,000-foot vertical gain), then up the Jomsom Trail to the Tibetan plateau, 115 miles away. It was ambitious, but doable. I've actually always been very athletic, but only discovered long-distance hiking on this global adventure. The farthest I'd walked in one shot—a hut-to-hut trek in Tasmania—was 56 miles, but I was certain I could manage in Nepal, even with residual Tim Tams added on to my belly.

I spent two days getting permits, rain pants, and plenty of film, plus a visa extension and new soles for my hiking boots. The day before I left, Rabindra took me shopping to stock up on trail food and snacks—packets of noodle soups, giant chocolate bars, teabags, and peanuts. During the final preparations, he calculated how much money I would need, figuring that thirty dollars (1,500 rupees) would be fine for thirteen days. That may not sound like much, but local meals typically cost less than one dollar and budget lodging averaged fifty cents per night. I brought forty dollars just to be safe and left my spare cash and traveler's checks with Rabindra for safekeeping.

At six o'clock on a Tuesday morning, I pointed my resoled boots toward the mountains and covered the estimated six-hour trek in half as long, propelled by a great sense of excitement. I come from a place where mountains top out at 6,200 feet and snow lasts just a few months a year. In Nepal, I was walking among 26,000-foot peaks that had been frozen solid for *millions* of years. And because Pokhara is situated right next to the Annapurna range, it only took a short walk to be in the midst of these giants.

From my pillow at five o'clock the next morning, I could see the fishtail peak of Machapuchare, glowing golden yellow under the sun's first rays—an exhilarating sight. The mountain looked deceptively close, like the full moon on a cloudless night, and I was on the mud-packed trail heading toward it less than an hour later. I am definitely not a morning person, but these views were enough to pull me out of bed by sunrise eleven days in a row. I wound my way out of Ghandruk just as the villagers were waking up and beginning their daily chores: scooping yak dung off stone pathways (for fertilizer), collecting buckets of water from a river, and sweeping the steps and dirt gardens around their gray stone homes. On a terraced hillside, an older man and his two oxen plowed a field for planting rice.

I made my way through forests of rhododendron trees and marigolds, and up a twisty, narrow path overlooking Modi Valley. Up ahead, I caught glimpses of the Annapurna glaciers—dramatic, soaring ice masses that appeared to slice through the heavens. That feeling of wonder, lying dormant within me for so long, was finally being rekindled and it was a thrilling sensation. Although I was tired and still had 7,000 feet of climbing to reach Annapurna Base Camp (ABC) and another eleven days of hiking to go, but everything seemed possible and within reach.

Then, suddenly and without warning, my plans collapsed like a fallen cake. That evening—just the second night of this solo trek—I realized I had a major dilemma. I was staying at the Moon Light Lodge, run by a woman rumored to have the best pizza on the trail to ABC. After hiking thirteen miles along torturously steep terrain, not only did I want one, I thought I deserved one. Everything had seemed very expensive those first two days, though, and I was beginning to wonder whether I could afford it. I tucked myself into a corner of the dining room with a menu and my crinkled rupees and began counting.

Let's see, pizzas cost $4 (plain) to $4.50 (with the works), I thought, *and according to my calculations, I have $34 to spend over the next eleven days. That leaves me with just...subtract 3 and add a zero...$3.09 per day.* Even if I skimped, that was barely enough to survive, considering only two basic meals plus accommodations were averaging $3.40 daily. Worse, though, pizza was out.

So I filled my stomach with black tea, noodle soup, and one-eighth of a chocolate bar, and spent the night watching other trekkers eat themselves silly. For six hours, it was the same scenario: someone ordered a pizza and after devouring it, the person announced it was one of the best pizzas he or she had eaten "in months," "ever," "in Asia," "since I've been traveling the last two years." It was torture. But my back was stiff, my legs ached, and I was too tired to go out walking to escape, even when the pizza smells rose, like heat, into my guest room.

I lay in bed that night pondering what to do, weighing options and dreaming up alternatives, then decided that after traveling so far, for so long—through nine countries over the course of seventeen months—there was simply no chance I was turning around. I suppose I could have appealed to guesthouse owners for handouts, but locals have their own worries and struggles, and I didn't want to add to them. Or I could have asked another trekker for money or food, but pride prevented me from seriously considering this option.

I didn't hold Rabindra responsible. His intentions were good. He just hadn't been hiking in years and things change, even when they're in your own backyard. It was my mistake for not doing more research, so I would just have to accept the consequences. *Really, this isn't that dramatic,* I thought to myself. *After all, pilgrims, monks, and Muslims fast. I'm sure I can handle it for a short time. Besides, I've heard it can be healthy—clears the mind and purges toxins from the body.*

So I continued on my trek and over the next eleven days, I hiked and slipped and scrambled and climbed my way up to 14,000 feet, then down and up another 9,000 feet, over rugged, undulating terrain—the most strenuous hiking I've ever done. The trails led me down into gorges, up steep muddy slopes, over wobbly suspension bridges, and across whitewater streams on shaky fallen logs. They also took me along narrow ledges and across snowfields, which I had to cross quickly due to potential avalanches, and at the end of one grueling day, up a rock staircase that had 1,782 steps, according to a trekker who'd counted. It should go without saying that hunger came often, and ferociously. I tried to satisfy my empty stomach with fried potatoes and fried rice, the only dishes I could afford, or my noodle soups and trail food. I had my weak moments and my strong moments. Some mornings I was charged up by my surroundings—the sunrise over glaciated peaks, the electric blue skies, the crisp air and, one day, the sight of a thundering avalanche that whisked wildflowers, boulders, and ice into the valley below. The

---

The best thing about the inn food was that it was all fresh, cooked to order. Someone was always chopping veggies in the corner of a Nepali kitchen, while some form of *chapati* bread puffed in the outdoor oven. Purna and Ram ate *dal-bhat* twice a day, but my favorite was Swiss *rosti*, a potato pancake stuffed with diced onions, carrots, celery, and cabbage. I found that the inns often looked poor and shabby from a distance, but were clean, orderly, and comfortable when you entered. I never went to bed hungry, cold, or dirty.

—Virginia Barton Brownback,
"A Walk in the Annapurnas,"
Travelers' Tales Nepal

scenery got my adrenaline pumping and not even an empty stomach could slow me down.

Other times, I was cursing so much I could barely breathe. Day four—and already several meals behind—I hiked with Ian, a Welshman I had met on the trail to ABC. After so much time spent walking alone, it was wonderful to have company, not to mention a great diversion from thoughts of food. Soft-spoken, quick-witted, and compassionate, Ian was one of the nicest people I'd met in months and by far the best-looking guy I'd seen in a year and a half. And he was a real gentleman.

But by afternoon, I decided I hated him. Ian was practically skipping along the trail, while my legs felt like two tubes of wet sand, made worse by a pack that seemed to have doubled in weight throughout the day. Ian walked fast and I pushed to keep up, my competitive spirit displacing the emptiness in my stomach and fueling each step I took. For a moment, I was tempted to tell him what was slowing me down, maybe even let him cover dinner, if he offered. But I just couldn't. It was too embarrassing and besides, I had made my choice to continue despite the situation, and I felt I needed to stick to those terms.

The next morning was a long, painful trudge. We hiked for four hours up (and, it seemed, rarely down) a path that cut through dense bamboo and rhododendron forest, where gray monkeys chattered at us. Ian and I stopped for lunch at a teahouse and I tried to be as cheerful as possible, while I nibbled potato leftovers from breakfast—by then, my stomach had shrunk so much that I couldn't eat a whole meal in one sitting—and sipped yet another cup of black tea. Meanwhile, I watched Ian devour a beautiful, fat piece of buttered corn bread and several plates of *dhal bhat*, a lentil-and-rice dish. I vowed to hike alone the next day.

As if lunch hadn't been torturous enough, everything I saw around me either was food or reminded me of food. Luscious strawberry bushes—with unripe, green fruit—grew alongside the trails, and every guesthouse we passed advertised Snickers, Mars bars, and Mexican food. As I climbed high above the Modi Valley, a thick fog induced visions of cotton candy and the river below looked the color of milk chocolate. On the opposite side of the river, green plants growing out of crevices in a sheer cliff resembled crisp heads of lettuce.

Since guesthouse supplies were hauled in by yak or on foot, prices rose with the altitude. Inevitably, so did my hunger. By the time I reached Annapurna Base Camp at 12,500 feet, lodging fees had doubled, food costs had nearly tripled, and my stomach rumblings could practically drown out the sound of avalanches. I couldn't afford fried potatoes or rice, so I ate another noodle soup and two packets of peanuts (meaning twenty-four peanuts, total—I counted). If it hadn't been for the prices, I would have stayed in that big ice bowl, surrounded by tall, serrated peaks and terminal moraine, watching snowboarders and sunsets and butterflies.

I was feeling dreamy and didn't know if it was fatigue, starvation, or the thinning air that had put me in that state. It followed me everywhere I went over the next few days, from the Annapurna Base Camp back down along the Modi Valley, with its strawberry bushes and chocolate-colored river, to Tatopani, then north toward the Tibetan Plateau through brown-colored mountains that resembled upside-down sugar cones. By then my knees ached and my feet were swollen from the steep, rocky terrain, but I was past the halfway mark so there was no way I would turn

> A few more days and a few thousand feet higher, the altitude was hitting me hard. As I lay in my tent, word spread among the porters of my failing health. Quickly, Kharel the cook came to my door with an offering—a little plate full of locally grown bite-sized roasted potatoes, topped with ginger, garlic, and sprinkled with salt. Despite my upset stomach and dizziness, I dutifully ate what was offered. Miraculously, within minutes, I was back on my feet and feeling fine. The Nepalese are very knowledgeable mountain people, and I was grateful for the food remedy from Kharel the wonder cook.
>
> —Lisel Doreste, "Kharel"

around. Luckily, the scenery kept me going as I made my way north along Kaligandaki's dry riverbed, passing through stone villages with colorful prayer flags and Tibetan temples, as well as big cornfields and clear views of the towering, snow-capped mountains.

I arrived in a village called Kalopani around dinnertime, day eight, with my pants drooping down to my hipbones. I was being stripped of all body fat—every Tim Tam, *martabak*, and *mysorepak* that had set up camp on my waistline, as well as every fruit, vegetable, rice dish, and loaf of bread that I'd enjoyed over the last month. *Purges toxins,* I reminded myself. *No more MSG, caffeine, and artificial preservatives. No ammonium bicarbonates or potassium sorbates. Purge those red and green and yellow food colorings! Plus the mounds and mounds of palm sugar and butter—gone!—not to mention all that fried dough I've eaten lately. So unhealthy. Just follow that trail and purge those toxins! Focus on the mountains and keep on moving. Keep...on...moving!*

The landscape around Kalopani was so dramatic that it seemed unreal. Out of one bedroom window, 23,000-foot mountains glowed under the setting sun, as it reflected off ice packed into their crevices. Through another window, I caught a glimpse of snowy, chiseled mountains that rose into the air like steps, as if beckoning me toward them. And out my door, a smooth, slate-like wall of rock culminated in knife-edge points 9,000 feet above me. When my neck began to ache from looking up, I watched women working the rice fields around the village and listened to mules clicking along a cobblestone street. The sound of their hooves reminded me of popcorn crackling against the lid of a pot.

My wallet and waistline were definitely shrinking. I was down to $8.50 and probably a good ten pounds lighter. I could also feel my willpower dissolving as stories about food began filtering down the trail. The farther north I went, talk among travelers turned more and more to Marpha, a village on the Jomsom Trail, and more specifically to the apple pie served at guesthouses there. Trekkers I met seemed less concerned with hot showers and solariums than with which guesthouses served more hot custard on their apple crumbles. And boy, I knew what they meant. They were speaking my language now.

I arrived in Marpha day nine, after six hours hiking along a riverbed past Dhauligiri, whose peak, at one point, stood one-and-a-half vertical miles above me. I was impressed by that as much as I was awed by the amount of yellow custard the cook at Neeru Guesthouse put on my apple crumble. Yes, I had broken down and ordered a big slice. It was a moment of weakness and I knew it meant no food my last day on the trail, but maybe I could sell a roll of film or my rain pants. I just couldn't face another plate of potatoes. That's all I'd had—potatoes, potatoes, and lots of rice. Those were the cheapest things on every menu, so I had potatoes for breakfast and rice for dinner. I bulked it up with ketchup. But not that night! No, that night, I sat in the dining room for an hour, chewing the crumble slowly and letting the flavors linger on my tongue until they had found every taste bud at least twice. Then I stashed the last bite in my cheek until it began to taste sour.

Drugged, that's how I felt. My hunger, which had once nourished and propelled me, was just tempting and toying with me—or torturing me. My second-to-last day hiking, I had a horrible revelation that nearly turned me off food altogether. As I was preparing the last of my noodle soups, I realized those black things floating around weren't just specks of teapot debris or dehydrated vegetables. They were dozens of freeloading, shriveled-up bugs. I checked the expiration date and discovered that my soups—"Good price for you, Auntie"—had expired four years ago. I felt nauseated thinking I'd eaten eight of these infested soups on this trip. Not only that, they had often been the main source of nourishment during my skimpy meals. That's re-PUL-sive!

As a consolation, I used my last rupees to buy a Snickers bar and then climbed up a hill overlooking the Tibetan village of Kagbeni, where I was staying. I found a spot where I could look out over the stunning, green wheat fields, which whispered and swayed in a strong breeze. The dry riverbed next to Kagbeni wound out of sight, like a long string of licorice, heading deep into forbidden Mustang country. In the far distance were brown, fluted hillsides with glacial mountains as a backdrop. Here, I sat on a rock and ate *The Snickers.*

Out of food, money, and energy, I decided to cut the trekking time, though not the distance, a day short. I spent the last day covering 16 miles (a ten-hour walk), making my way north along a pilgrimage route to a temple at Muktinath and then retracing my steps south. During the final hours of my hike, I walked along a totally exposed mountainside to Kagbeni and then across a wide and dry, rocky riverbed to Jomsom. The winds in this region are fierce in the afternoon and gale-force gusts nearly flattened me. Walking took all the energy I could muster, and by the time I reached Jomsom, where I would fly out the next day, I had torn muscles around both knees from struggling to step forward.

I told the lodge owner at Rita Guesthouse I wouldn't be eating dinner—"upset stomach," I said—and retreated to my room. As I lay in bed reflecting on the trip, I realized that over the course of twelve days, I had skipped fourteen meals and survived merely on rice and potatoes, plus my infested soups and chocolate bars as fillers, and that whopping big bowl of apple crumble. In the end, I figured I'd lost fifteen pounds, two love handles, and my (face) cheeks, and developed Olympic legs. But I'd gained a greater appreciation of food, a transformative experience, and an amazing sense of satisfaction from having completed the 115-mile hike. I fell asleep that night dreaming about cornbread and apple crumble and about all the food I would eat as soon as I arrived back in Pokhara.

Kari Bodnarchuk is the author of Rwanda: A Country Torn Apart *and* Kurdistan: Region Under Siege, *two children's books in a World in Conflict series. Her work has appeared in the* Denver Post, Islands, Backpacker, The Christian Science Monitor, The Greatest Adventures of All Time, The Unsavvy Traveler: Women's Comic Tales of Catastrophe, Travelers' Tales Australia, *and* Gutsy Women. *From her home in Boston, she is currently writing* Tales From A-Broad, *about her eighteen-month solo trip around the world.*

DIANE SELKIRK

✦ ✦ ✦

Bonito *Mañana*

Promises, promises.

ANOTHER GLORIOUS SUN SETS OVER THE COBALT OCEAN. Dolphins are swimming by and Evan and I are satiated with my first personally caught fish. I had been fishing for months without success. An old fisherman taught me the technique but I was beginning to doubt it; perhaps it was too simplistic. Reel out a heavy line with a lure, any lure, any color, on a wire leader, until it skips on the surface. Then ignore it. I added the call "Here fishy, fishy!" in the hope of encouraging the fish. But nothing ever went for my line, not a single hit. Tonight though, as our luminous sails are filled with a warm breeze and *Ceilydh* rushes down the face of each wave, I am finally a fisherman.

We are enroute to our second Mexican port of call, Bahia Magdalena. We are weeks behind a self-imposed schedule and finally we just accept *mañana* time. Happiness, friendship, and good food, kept us in the tiny fishing village of Turtle Bay longer than anticipated. From now on this will be the way of our journey.

The evening before leaving we chatted over *cervezas* with our fisherman friends Ignacio and Alfredo. The evening sun was warm on our faces as animated conversation filled our cockpit. Hand gestures, combined with fragments of English and Spanish, augmented by a dictionary and punctuated with laughter was how we talked. On the shore across from our gently bobbing boat was the dusty village. The purple and white church stood out in the clear desert air, contrasted against the endless shades of browns, reds, and tans. Ignacio tried to convince us to stay, promising a bonito fish *mañana*. Ah! We had learned about *mañana*; *mañana* may never come and if it does it is never the one that is promised. So we stayed resolute. Previously, our departure was delayed by the promise of that same bonito, "dot with butter and lime and wrap in foil, when you eat this fish you will know why you have come to Mexico," Ignacio had confided in us.

Midmorning, as promised, Ignacio and Alfredo bumped their fishing panga up against our anchored boat. A silver-and-blue-striped fish was selected and extracted from a wet sack. It was not a bonito, they explained; they would bring us that *mañana*. This was a sierra. Alfredo began to filet the fish. With three deft strokes he held up the glistening white flesh. Examining it carefully, he pulled out translucent bones with rusty pliers. Ignacio handed the two filets to me saying, "Brush it with

The exquisite taste, delectable texture, and extremely white meat of the bonito make it the most coveted of tunas. Marked by slanted, dark stripes along its back, it travels vast distances in search of food, spending most of its time in the warm waters between Mexico and Southern California. Other common names for the bonito include bonehead, Laguna tuna, magneto, striped tuna, and ocean bonito.

—LB

olive oil and garlic and barbeque. Cook it very hot at first. You will like this very much. Tomorrow the bonito!"

The next morning we strolled through the dirt streets and gazed through dusty shop windows. Children led us from place to place as we used careful Spanish to ask for directions. The last stop was the grocery store. As it was lit only by the sun streaming through the open door and the clouded windows, it took a moment for our eyes to adjust. The shelves held random items: hardware, candies, powdered milk, firecrackers. Near the windows were boxes for produce. We selected from what there was: limes, avocados, cucumbers, and onions. At the back in the gloom, the flies surrounded the meat and cheese and we were glad fishermen had befriended us. On the way back to the boat a smiling Ignacio ran up to us. He told us he had left a surprise on our boat. "Break off the tails and boil them for a few minutes, eat with tortillas and salsa."

"The bonito?" I asked confused.

Later that evening, with our bellies filled with Ignacio and Alfredo's gift of lobster, we watched the stately procession of a Quince Años celebration. Though not a part of large Mexican city life anymore, it was still alive in this small west coast Baja town. Ignacio's niece had turned fifteen. She was dressed in a beautiful white gown and was attended by fifteen teenagers. The celebration had a formal beginning. The group danced traditional Spanish dances, then the young woman was presented to the crowd. To symbolize the passing of her childhood she tossed a doll to a group of waiting girls. Then she was presented with her first pair of high-heeled shoes. The entire town seemed to fill the hall as the ceremony ended and the party began. A local band, crammed up on stage with dozens of extra people, began to fill the hall with a Latin beat. The locals seemed intent on including us in the activity; teaching me to dance, insisting we try the food, telling us 3:30 A.M. was too early to leave.

It wasn't until late the next day that Ignacio and Alfredo arrived. "This is ceviche. Today there was no fishing." In our cockpit we ate the raw tuna marinated in lime and spices, then finished the meal with my homemade chocolate chip cookies, the first they had ever tasted.

"Tomorrow we will bring a bonito and you will give us more cookies." I had to explain that I was out of chocolate chips, and didn't think I would find any in town. It didn't matter; there would still be a bonito *mañana*.

The days continued and our friendship grew. Our Spanish expanded and conversation became more detailed. "What is it like to travel the world by sailboat?" they wanted to know. "What is it like to be a fisherman in a tiny Mexican village?" we wondered. Each day there was a new fish, a new recipe, an invitation to shore, a visit in our cockpit. Each day we said we should leave, we had friends waiting for us farther south. "But you can't leave, you have never tried this fish before and *mañana* we will bring the bonito." *Mañana* came but the bonito never did; finally the day arrived when we knew we had to go.

We feasted together that last night. Lobster tacos with thick gua-camole that spilled out and stained our clothes. Sour ceviche with crunchy carrots that fell off our crackers as we laughed. The air was filled with the sizzle and splatter of barbequeing fish. We drank cold, but rapidly warming, Tecate beer, and scooped up fresh salsa as we grabbed for the dictionary to find the words to express ideas or opinions. We would dart below to find small gifts for them, know-ing we would never forget our first Mexican fish and our first Mexican friends.

The next day when we left, Ignacio and Alfredo weren't on the bay. As I went through my routine of throwing out a fishing line, I thought of how it must be to make your life catching fish. I didn't even get a chance to say "Here fishy, fishy!" before zing! Evan yelled that I had a hit, a hard hit. My rod was in disarray as I excitedly began to reel the fish in. I saw a flash of plump firm expanse, a tuna maybe. He was a fighter. In and out I played him. Evan waited, gaff at the ready, for when he tired. Suddenly the line was slack. Sadly I reeled in, knowing the awful truth. The fish had got away. My knot had come undone and with the fish went my lure and wire leader. My line was left in tangles. I decided the best way to untangle the line was to throw it back over the side and unwind until I hit new line. Out it went. We discovered that the line had broken, so we began to reel the line that was out back in on the end of the gaff. Then it happened: zing! Or rather, "We have a fish!" We reeled it in by hand slowly and laboriously.

This fish was new to us and very pretty: long and sleek with a white belly and blue top with dark blue stripes. We decided to cook it wrapped in foil and doted with butter and lime. It tasted good with firm pink flesh that looked and cooked like chicken. As we sat in the cockpit and the sky began to glow, I thumbed through my fish identification guide.

The fish I had caught was a bonito.

Diane Selkirk spent six years traveling and living aboard her thirty-foot sailboat Ceilydah *with her husband. After sailing from Vancouver, British Columbia through Mexico, Central America, and the Western Caribbean, she is now settled in Annapolis, Maryland. She plans to continue traveling once the bank and boat declare themselves ready.*

HELEN BAROLINI

⋆ ⋆ ⋆

In Pursuit of the
Great White Truffle

Can you ever match the rapture of the first time?

IT'S FALL. TIME FOR ME TO THINK OF TRUFFLES AND ITALY. IF I could make a trip back each year to Italy, where I was married and once lived, it would be in the autumn when truffle season arrives. When I return to Italy, it is to immerse myself, like a pilgrim gaining indulgences, in the Italian life and food I so loved: truffles are my calling.

It happens that my middle daughter Susanna is married to an Italian artist and lives near Urbino, which is not only an exquisite hill-town and the birthplace of Raphael, but also most opportunely situated in a zone where the white truffle is found.

A white truffle, currently priced at about $65–$90 an ounce, is something worth pursuing. The Romans knew and valued truffles, ascribing aphrodisiac powers to them and dedicating the tuber (*tartufo bianco*) to Venus. "Keep your grain," Juvenal wrote, "but send us your truffles."

One year my youngest daughter, Niki, and I timed our visit to Susi for the fall truffle season. We drove our rented car East across Italy's mountainous spine toward the Marche region passing through Umbria where the black truffle reigns. The black truffle has its own flavor and mystique and, being denser and less perishable

165

than the rarer white, it can be cooked. Whites are never cooked. Black and white are different and each in its own way superb. But my gastronomic memory is precise: it is the white truffle that enraptured me when I first had it in Rome, grated over freshly made noodles. I remember that the truffle looked like nothing more than a knobby brown golf ball. But the fragrance! An aroma was released—distinctive, woodsy, and earthy—that has been my touchstone for gastronomical bliss ever since.

An ancient saying has it that "those who wish to lead virtuous lives should abstain from truffles." I believe it. With what they cost, weighing in like emeralds, one could be led to beg, borrow, or steal to obtain a respectable amount. King Umberto of Italy was said to be fond of a salad made of thinly sliced white truffle with a few greens and nasturtium blossoms, an aesthetic ultimate.

Living outside New York I would be tempted every so often to go into the city to a shop of Italian imports and plunk down what seemed a huge wad of bills for a "truffle just arrived from Italy." It would look like a truffle, it would cost like a truffle, but when the moment of truth came with the

---

The Saturday market in Alba is well attended. The olfactory blast of fungi dirt immediately hits us as we enter the large white tent hosting the truffle sales. The intoxicating smell of the white truffle is heady and rich and stays with us all day, as though it has seeped into our pores. Rows of tables with weighed out white and black truffles circumvent the room with each truffle sitting on a piece of paper indicating its price in lire. Larger truffles are stored for safety under bell jar lids, the owners enticing buyers by lifting the lid and offering a whiff of the "white diamond." We purchased our own *tartufo bianco* for thirty dollars, and the odor would not be contained in its bag; it is as though truffle perfume is a living thing.

—Marcia Hewitt Johnson,
"In Search of Truffles"

grating, it would be utterly disappointing—a mere wisp of scent and taste.

Once Susi located a noted truffle hunter who was said to have concocted some secret balsamic elixir which perfectly preserved them out of season. Wanting to indulge me, she sent me a tiny brown lump floating in the liquid of a small vial marked *tartufo bianco*. It was not a truffle but a *truffa*—a swindle. The lump was soft and spongy from its balsamic bath, and tasteless, worthless.

It seemed clear that the truffle must be had where it is found and had fresh—dug from the earth that very day.

So it was October when Niki and I drove in sight of that enchanting vision, the twin fairy tale towers of Urbino's Ducal Palace. White truffles were already in the town's speciality shops. And I learned that in local jargon, a *tartufo* is someone who turns up when there is something choice to eat or a bottle of wine has been opened. I thought, if I can't find one, perhaps I can be one.

Susi helped me lay the plan: the goal was to get the truffle as fresh as possible and use it immediately. "There's a mushroom festival this Sunday in Fermignano," my son-in-law Nevio told us. "That will be the place to find the truffle hunters."

Fermignano is a little country town in the plain below Urbino, one of those usual, pleasant but seemingly unremarkable towns that Italy abounds in; one in which one passes through, not thinking twice of it. But Fermignano merited a second thought for it was the birthplace of Bramante and the long tree-lined avenue, fronted by small houses in gardens, which led into the main colonnaded piazza, was named for him. On this day the main square was filled with country carts festooned with such wayside flowers as tall golden coreopsis and the wild blue asters, called *settembrini* in Italy because they start blooming in September. It was the mushroom market in full sway: hundreds of varieties, the deadly and the edible from all over Italy, filled the tables along with displays of beehives and honey pots and the sweets made from them. It was a charming scene of country life in a small-town market square and the sort of thing I love about Italy, but we were on a serious mission and there wasn't time to linger over mushrooms or honey-drops.

Nevio spotted Ivo, a sturdy countryman whom he knew slightly and, in the low tones one might use to conduct an exchange of state secrets, asked where we could get a white truffle. *"Ah, gia,"* responded Ivo, "you'll want Quinto." We followed our man Ivo down the backstreets until he stopped in front of double wooden doors sealed with a chain. Across the narrow street, the inevitable know-it-all neighbor came out of her house to say, "Are you looking for Quinto? He's not here. Quinto is out with some fellow from Turin."

Quinto, it seems, was into big business. Someone from the northern Piedmont region, where the town of Alba is the celebrated locale of the best-known Italian white truffles, had come to the lesser-known (and much less expensive) zone in the Marches region to make a buy. With Alba truffles selling at exorbitant rates, the man from Turin must have realized that he could get white truffles cheaper in Fermignano and take them back to the Piedmont to sell as the renowned whites of Alba.

Obviously, Quinto was into a bigger deal than my wish for one white truffle to have with noodles that evening. Having missed Quinto, we were leaving the piazza when Ivo came up with another man who said he had dug truffles that very morning. *Benissimo!* This time we followed by car as he drove to his home on the outskirts of town.

We were invited into the darkened sitting room off the entry hall of his silent, dimly-lit house. He went off and we stood there waiting, staring at a round table in the center of the room with a scale on it. The man reappeared carrying something wrapped in a handkerchief. As he unfolded it, divine aroma filled the place: it was certainly a truffle.

"It stinks in here," said Niki in English.

"How much," I whispered to Susi who passed it on to Nevio who asked the man. Forty thousand lire per *etto*, the man said. I couldn't believe the low price but, from my years of marketing experience in Italy, knew not to show my eagerness.

"How do we know it's fresh?" I asked to indicate I was no novice.

"Ma, signora, non si sente?" Well, can't you smell it, the man

retorted more than reasonably. Indeed I could, it was heaven. But courteously, to reassure me, he repeated, "I dug it up this morning."

It was Sunday and not unreasonable that a working man would use his day off to hunt truffles which commanded such prices in such a short season. He weighed it on the scale and it came to 550 grams, a trifle over a half-etto. It cost twenty-two thousand lire, about $18.00 then.

"How shall I keep it?" I asked him.

"Keep it wrapped, keep it from the heat, and put it in the refrigerator if you don't use it right away."

We drove off and rushed the truffle home, burying it in rice in a glass jar; long ago I had learned that the rice would then absorb the aroma and be the makings of a superb risotto. We secluded the jar in the deepest recesses of the fridge.

That night we prepared fresh *tagliatelle* and as soon as they were about to be drained, I got the truffle out, gently wiped it with a slightly damp cloth to remove any earth that might still cling to it, and while imbibing that wonderful odor (while Susi's five-year-old son screamed, "Phew! I don't want that!") I grated the precious tuber over the pasta.

But wait—it wasn't white. Somehow my memory had tricked me into thinking the truffle would look like paper-thin slivered almonds, even though I'd been reassured by no less of an authority than Elizabeth David whose *Italian Food* had long reigned in my kitchen, that white truffles "are in reality a dirty brownish color on the outside, beige inside."

In fact, while Nevio raved and said, "Susi, this is wonderful, we should do it more often. What a delicate taste!" I kept to myself the knowledge that, though tasty and sublimely fragrant, this truffle was not the one I had tasted for the first time so many years ago; the rapture was not the same. But then, is it ever?

Helen Barolini is the author of seven books, including The Dream Book, *for which she won an National Book Award,* Umbertina, *and more than fifty stories and essays, which have appeared in numerous publications and collections, including* Best American Essays.

PART FOUR

Is That on the Menu?

CHITRITA BANERJI

What Bengali Widows Cannot Eat

*A daughter struggles with
the power of a culture.*

MY FATHER DIED AT THE BEGINNING OF A PARTICULARLY RADIANT
and colorful spring. Spring in Bengal is teasing and elusive, secret
yet palpable, waiting to be discovered. The crimson and scarlet of
palash and shimul flowers post the season's banners on high trees.
Compared to the scented flowers of the summer and monsoon—
jasmine, beli, chameli, kamini, gardenias, all of which are white—
these scentless spring flowers are utterly assertive with the one asset
they have: color. My father, who was a retiring, unassuming man,
took great pleasure in their flaunting, shameless reds. When I
arrived in Calcutta for his funeral, I was comforted by the sight of
the flowers in full bloom along the road from the airport.

That first evening back home, my mother and I sat out on our
roof, talking. As darkness obscured all colors, the breeze became
gusty, laden with unsettling scents from out-of-season potted flowers on neighboring roofs.

My mother had always been dynamic, forceful, efficient: the
family's principal breadwinner for nearly thirty years, she had risen
above personal anxiety and ignored social disapproval to allow me,
alone, young, and unmarried, to pursue my studies in the United
States. Yet overnight, she had been transformed into the arche-

typal Bengali widow—meek, faltering, hollow-cheeked, sunken-eyed, the woman in white from whose life all color and pleasure must evaporate.

During the thirteen days of mourning that precede the Hindu rituals of *shraddha* (last rites) and the subsequent *niyambhanga* (literally, the breaking of rules), all members of the bereaved family live ascetically on one main meal a day of rice and vegetables cooked together in an earthen pot with no spices except sea salt, and no oil, only a touch of ghee. The sanction against oil embraces its cosmetic use too, and for me, the roughness of my mother's parched skin and hair made her colorless appearance excruciating. But what disturbed me most was the eagerness with which she seemed to be embracing the trappings of bereavement. Under the curious, observant, and critical eyes of female relatives, neighbors, and visitors, she appeared to be mortifying her flesh almost joyfully, as if those thirteen days were a preparation for the future. As if it is utterly logical for a woman to lose her self and plunge into a life of ritual suffering once her husband is dead.

Hindu tradition in Bengal holds that the widow must strive for purity through deprivation. In contrast with the bride, who is dressed in red and, if her family's means permit, decked out in gold jewelry, the widow, regardless of her wealth and status, is drained of color. Immediately after her husband's death, other women wash the *sindur*, a vermilion powder announcing married status, from the parting in the widow's hair. All jewelry is removed, and she exchanges her colored or patterned sari for the permanent, unvarying uniform of the *thaan*, borderless yards of blank white cotton. Thus transformed, she remains, for the rest of her life, the pallid symbol of misfortune, the ghostly twin of the Western bride, dressed in virginal white, drifting down the aisle towards happiness.

As recently as fifty years ago, widows were also forced to shave their heads as part of a socially prescribed move towards androgyny. Both of my grandfather's sisters were widowed in their twenties: my childhood memories of them are of two nearly identical creatures wrapped in shroud-like white who emerged from their village a couple of times a year and came to visit us in the city. Whenever the *thaan* covering their heads slipped, I would be overcome with an urge to rub my hands over their prickly scalps that resembled the spherical, yellow, white-bristled flowers of the kadam tree in our garden.

Until the Hindu Widow Remarriage Act was passed in 1856, widows were forbidden to marry for a second time. But for more than a hundred years after the act became law, it did not translate into any kind of widespread social reality (unlike the 1829 edict abolishing the burning of widows on the same pyre as their dead husbands—the infamous practice of *suttee*). Rural Bengali households were full of widows who were no more than children, because barely pubescent girls often found themselves married to men old enough to be their fathers.

It was not until the morning before the actual *shraddha* ceremony that I was forced to confront the cruelest of the rules imposed on the widow by the Sanskrit *shastras*, the body of rules and rituals of Hindu life to which have been added innumerable folk beliefs. One of my aunts took me aside and asked if my mother had made up her mind to give up eating fish and meat—*amish*, non-vegetarian food, forbidden for widows. With a sinking heart, I realized that the image of the widow had taken such a hold of my mother that she was only too likely to embrace a vegetarian diet—all the more so because she had always loved fish and had been renowned for the way she cooked it. If I said nothing, she would never again touch those wonders of the Bengali kitchen—*shorshe-ilish, maacher jhol, galda chingrir malaikari, lau-chingri, doi-maach, maacher kalia*. It was an unbearable thought.

The vegetarian stricture is not considered a hardship in most regions of India where the majority, particularly the Brahmins and some of the upper castes, have always been vegetarians. But Bengal is blessed with innumerable rivers crisscrossing a fertile delta, and it is famed for its rice and its fish. Even Brahmins have lapsed in Bengal by giving in to the regional taste for fish, which plays a central part in both the diet and the culinary imagination of the country. Fish, in its ubiquity, symbolism, and variety, becomes, for the Bengali widow, the finest instrument of torture.

Several other items are forbidden to widows simply because of their associations with *amish*. *Puishak*, for instance, a spinach-like leafy green often cooked with small shrimps or the fried head of a hilsa fish, is disallowed. So are onion and garlic, which were eschewed by most Hindus until the last century because of their association with meat-loving Muslims. They are further supposed to have lust-inducing properties, making them doubly unsuitable for widows. Lentils, a good source of protein in the absence of meat, are also taboo—a stricture which might stem from the widespread practice of spicing them with chopped onion.

Social historians have speculated that these dietary restrictions served a more sinister and worldly function than simply that of moving a widow towards a state of purity: they would also lead to malnutrition, thus reducing her lifespan. A widow often has property, and her death would inevitably benefit someone—her sons, her siblings, her husband's family. And in the case of a young widow, the sooner she could be dispatched to the next world, the less the risk of any moral transgression and ensuing scandal.

My grandmother lived the last twenty-seven of her eighty-two years as a widow, obeying every stricture imposed by rules and custom. The memory of her bleak, pinched, white-robed widowhood intensified my determination to prevent my mother from embracing a similar fate. I particularly remember a scene from my early teens. I was the only child living with an extended family of parents, uncles and aunts—and my grandmother. It had been a punishingly hot and dry summer. During the day, the asphalt on the streets would melt, holding on to my sandals as I walked. Night brought sweat-drenched sleeplessness and the absorbing itchiness of prickly heat. Relief would come only with the eagerly awaited monsoon.

The rains came early one morning—dark, violent, lightning-streaked, fragrant, and beautiful. The cook rushed to the market and came back with a big hilsa fish which was cut up and fried, the crispy, flavorful pieces served at lunchtime with *khichuri*, rice and *dhal* cooked together. This is the traditional way to celebrate the arrival of the monsoon. Though I knew my grandmother did not eat fish, I was amazed on this occasion to see that she did not touch either the *khichuri* or the battered slices of aubergine or the fried potatoes. These were vegetarian items, and I had seen her eat them before on other wet and chilly days. This time, she ate, in her usual solitary spot, *luchis*, a kind of fried bread, that looked stale, along with some equally unappetizing cold, cooked vegetables.

Why? I asked in outrage. And my mother explained that this was because of a rare coincidence: the rains had arrived on the first day of Ambubachi, the three-day period in the Bengali month of Asharh that, according to the almanac, marks the beginning of the rainy season. The ancients visualized this as the period of the earth's receptive fertility, when the summer sun vanishes, the skies open and mingle with the parched land to produce a red or brown fluid flow of earth and water, nature's manifestation of menstruating femininity. How right then for widows to suffer more than usual at such a time. They were not allowed to cook during the three-day period, and, although they were allowed to eat some foods that had been prepared in advance, boiled rice was absolutely forbidden. Since nature rarely conforms to the calculations of the almanac, I had never noticed these Ambubachi strictures being observed on the long-awaited rainy day.

The almanac was an absolute necessity for conforming to the standards of ritual purity, and my grandmother consulted it assiduously. On the day before Ambubachi started, she would prepare enough *luchis* and vegetables for three midday meals. Sweet yogurt and fruit, mixed with *chira*—dried, flattened rice—were also permissible. That first night of monsoon, newly aware of the sanctions of Ambubachi, I went to look for my grandmother around dinner time. All she ate was a small portion of *kheer*, milk that had been boiled down to nearly solid proportions, and some pieces of mango. I had hoped she would at least be permitted one of her favorite evening meals—warm milk mixed with crushed mango pulp. But no. Milk cannot be heated, for the widow's food must not receive the touch of fire during Ambubachi. The *kheer*, a traditional way of preserving milk, had been prepared for her the day before.

✦

It is true that despite deprivations, household drudgery, and the imposition of many fasts, widows sometimes live to a great age, and the gifted cooks among them have contributed greatly to the range, originality, and subtlety of Hindu vegetarian cooking in Bengal. A nineteenth-century food writer once said that it was impossible to taste the full glory of vegetarian food unless your own wife became a widow. And Bengali literature is full of references to elderly widows whose magic touch can transform the most mundane or bitter of vegetables to nectar, whose subtlety with spices cannot be reproduced by other hands.

But however glorious these concoctions, no married woman envies the widow's fate. And until recently, most widows remained imprisoned within the austere bounds of their imposed diets. Even if they were consumed with temptation or resentment, fear of discovery and public censure were enough to inhibit them.

I knew the power of public opinion as I watched my mother during the day of the *shraddha*. My aunt, who had been widowed when fairly young, had been bold enough, with the encouragement of her three daughters, to continue eating fish.

But I knew that my mother and many of her cronies would find it far less acceptable for a woman in her seventies not to give up *amish* in her widowhood. As one who lived abroad, in America, I also knew that my opinion was unlikely to carry much weight. But I was determined that she should not be deprived of fish, and with the support of my aunt and cousins I prepared to fight.

The crucial day of the *niyambhanga*, the third day after the *shraddha*, came. On this day, members of the bereaved family invite all their relatives to lunch, and an elaborate meal is served, representing the transition between the austerity of mourning and normal life—for everyone except the widow. Since we wanted to invite many people who were not relatives, we arranged to have two catered meals, lunch and dinner, the latter for friends and neighbors. My mother seemed to recover some of her former energy that day, supervising everything with efficiency, attending to all the guests. But she hardly touched any food. After the last guest had left, and the caterers had packed up their equipment, leaving enough food to last us for two or three days, I asked her to sit down and eat dinner with me. For the first time since my father's death, the two of us were absolutely alone in the house. I told her I would serve the food; I would be the grown-up now.

She smiled and sat down at the table. I helped her to rice and *dhal*, then to two of the vegetable dishes. She held up her hand then. No more. I was not to go on to the fish. Silently, we ate. She asked for a little more rice and vegetables. I complied, then lifted a piece of rui fish and held it over her plate. Utter panic filled her eyes, and she shot anxious glances around the room. She told me, vehemently, to eat the fish myself.

It was that panic-stricken look around her own house, where she was alone with me, her daughter, that filled me with rage. I was determined to vanquish the oppressive force of ancient belief, reinforced by whatever model of virtue she had inherited from my grandmother. We argued for what seemed like hours, my voice rising, she asking me to be quiet for fear of the neighbors, until finally I declared that I would never touch any *amish* myself as long as she refused to eat fish. The mother who could not bear the thought of her child's deprivation eventually prevailed, though the woman still quaked with fear of sin and retribution.

I have won a small victory, but I have lost the bigger battle. My mother's enjoyment of food, particularly of fish, as well as her joyful exuberance in the kitchen where her labors produced such memorable creations, have vanished. Sometimes, as I sit and look at her, I see a procession of silent women in white going back through the centuries. They live as household drudges, slaves in the kitchen and the field; they are ostracized even in their own homes during weddings or other happy ceremonies—their very presence considered an invitation to misfortune.

In the dim corners they inhabit, they try to contain their hunger. Several times a year, they fast and pray and prepare spreads for priests and Brahmins, all in the hope of escaping widowhood in the next life. On the eleventh day of each moon, they deny themselves food and water and shed tears over their blameful fate, while women with husbands make a joyous ritual out of eating rice and fish. Their anguish and anger secreted in the resinous chamber of fear, these white-clad women make their wasteful progress towards death.

Chitrita Banerji grew up in Calcutta, received her Master's degree from Harvard University, and now lives in Cambridge, Massachusetts. She has written three books about the food and culture of Bengal—Life and Food in Bengal, Bengali Cooking: Seasons and Festivals, *and* The Hour of the Goddess: Memories of Women, Ritual, and Food in Bengal. *Her essays have appeared in many journals and have received awards at the Oxford Symposium on Food and Cookery. This story was first published in* Granta.

ISABEL ALLENDE

✦ ✦ ✦

Alligators and Piranhas

A jungle is one big mouth
and one big meal.

DEEP IN THE AMAZON, IN THE HEART OF SOUTH AMERICA, WHERE
the jungle can be so thick that if you wander two meters away from
the trail you are lost in Venusian vegetation, monkey is greatly
appreciated as food. I saw one skewered from mouth to anus roasting over a fire, burned to a crisp but still looking like a child.
Depending on the season, the texture is tough or tender, but the
flavor is always strong and sweetish. The jungle is an enormous, hot,
exhausting, mysterious labyrinth in which one can wander in circles forever. With its birdcalls, screeching animals, and stealthy foot-
falls, the jungle is never silent; it smells of moss, of dankness, and
sometimes you catch a mouthful of a clinging odor like rotted fruit.
To inexpert eyes, everything is green, but for the native, it is a
diverse and endlessly rich world: there are vines that gather liters
and liters of pure water to drink, bark that reduces fevers, leaves used
to treat diabetes, resins to close wounds, a milky sap that cures a
cough, rubber for affixing arrow points—in short, it is the largest
biogenetic preserve on the planet. The Indians use a poison extracted
from plants that they throw into the water to stun the fish. They
collect them when they float to the surface, then eat them without
danger because the poison quickly degrades.

After the waters of the Rio Negro and the Salomoes flow together, the river is called the Amazon. It is as broad as the sea in Normandy, a dark mirror when it is calm, terrifying when storms erupt. In a glass, water from the Rio Negro is a kind of amber color and has the delicate flavor of strong tea. At dawn, when the rising sun stains the horizon red, rosy dolphins come out to play, one of the few Amazonian fish that are not eaten, because the flesh is bitter and the skin unusable. The Indians harpoon them, nonetheless, and rip out their eyes and genitals to make into amulets for virility and fertility.

In that same warm river where the previous afternoon I had seen a couple of Russian tourists catch dozens of piranhas, I had swum naked. Although these fish have such a bad reputation, they normally do not attack people and, along with alligators, are useful for cleaning the water; they fulfill the same function as birds of prey: they eat carrion. They are delicious and, to some Brazilian palates, even aphrodisiac, but those tourists from Moscow had no intention of cooking them; they were fishing for the sport, catching them and throwing them back in the river. Some piranhas had taken the bait many times, leaving their mouths raw and bleeding. Like some of us humans, who keep tripping over the same stone in our path, the piranhas never learn.

In these same waters there are more than thirty kinds of stingrays, all very dangerous, and the river is also home to the legendary anaconda, largest of all water snakes, a prehistoric creature that can reach fifteen meters in length. It lies lethargically in the mud, waiting for its lunch to swim by in the form of a distracted fish. I was assured that they don't eat people, but in Malaysia I saw the photograph of a boa split open with a man's body inside. I have no reason to believe that the Amazonian anaconda would be any more considerate than its Asian cousin.

Alligators, another aphrodisiac dish of the region, are hunted at night. I went out in a canoe with an adolescent guide, a young Indian who openly laughed at my ignorance. The boat was equipped with a powerful battery-operated spotlight, which when turned on dazzled bats and huge, brightly colored butterflies—also the piranhas, which in their terror would leap right into the boat. To throw them back in the river, we picked them up very gingerly by the tail, because one bite from their terrible jaws can take off a finger. The Indian would beam his light in among the tree roots and, when he spotted a pair of red eyes, unhesitatingly jump into the water. You would hear a great thrashing sound, and a half minute later he would reemerge with a *jacaré*, an Amazon crocodile, he had caught bare-handed and was holding by the neck, if it was small, and with a cord around its jaws, if it was larger.

In one village, composed of a single extended family of Sateré Maué Indians, I tasted *jacaré* for the first time. It was beneath a shared palm roof hung with a few hammocks where several young Indians and a centenarian elder were resting, lost in the smoke of their tobacco. A half dozen children were running around naked, and when they saw me they scampered off to take refuge among the women, although a pair of mud-covered, skin-and-bone dogs came running up to sniff at me. One of the Indians, the only one who spoke a few words of Portuguese, showed me his humble belongings—arrows, a knife, some empty tin cans used as cook pots—and then led me to a small clearing in the vegetation where they had planted manioc, that miraculous root from which the Amazon peoples derive flour, tapioca, bread, and even a liquor for their celebrations. Out of curiosity, I walked over to the fire burning in a corner of the roofed area and found a crocodile a meter and a half long, quartered like a chicken, sadly roasting, its claws, teeth, eyes, and hide intact. Two piranhas were strung on a hook, along with something that resembled a muskrat; later, after a closer look, I realized it was a porcupine. I tried everything, of course: the jacaré tasted like dried and reconstituted codfish, the piranhas like pure smoke, and the porcupine like petrified pig—but I shouldn't judge indigenous cooking by that one limited experience.

Born in Peru, raised in Chile, and currently living in Northern California, Isabel Allende is the author of several books, including Daughter of Fortune, The House of the Spirits, Eva Luna, *and* Aphrodite: A Memoir of the Senses, *from which this story was excerpted.*

* [*] *

The Long Road

*A bicycle trip redefines the author's relationship
with food and her body.*

I CANNOT REALLY TELL YOU HOW THE WHOLE THING STARTED: THE concern with weight, the obsession with food, the panic over my body. It must have been after my first job at age fifteen. I worked at Frosty Burger, a fast food joint in the tradition of Dairy Queen. We served soft-serve ice cream that dripped if you did not lick it quickly and malts made in tins blended on lime-green mixers from the '50s that buzzed so loudly it was hard to hear a customer order. Out front were round, cement tables with matching benches. Customers ate their burgers and fries there and took an ice cream to go. My co-workers and I experimented daily — making and eating banana splits with churros, double-coned ice creams, triple-dipped ice creams, and various malts with names like pale chocolate, killer chocolate, and chocolate chip chocolate. I was fired and the weight came off naturally at first. Then I started helping it along.

Ten years later, my boyfriend Gary, our friend Bob, and I rode out of San Francisco bound for New York on a gray April morning. The trip had been a long time coming. Gary had twice cycled across the United States and was ready to go again. In high school, after I was fired, I had ridden my bike past Frosty Burger fantasizing about feeling strong and free, about traveling, about not turning around. So when Gary and I decided to relocate to New York, the trip fell into place. Bob joined us, thinking he would fly back to work whenever he had to.

The three of us pedaled down the California coastline past Santa Cruz and through Big Sur. We cycled with the Pacific Ocean on our right, while on our left chocolate-colored mountains with shifting shades of green seemed to roll along with us. We passed through Los Angeles and San Diego and climbed into the semi-desert mountains of Cleveland National Forest in rain and hail. When we plunged into the dry heat of the Imperial Valley, I felt the sun and wind on my face and felt strong and free, just as I had fantasized as a teenager. I knew that the decision to make this trip was the right one; I knew I would make it. But I had little idea of how it would challenge me or how it would change me.

The days had fallen into a pattern after almost a month on the road. Riding, eating, riding, eating, until we came to a town that looked like a good place to rest for the night. By the time we reached Sentinel, a dot on the Arizona map just off Interstate 8, we had ridden a solid seven hours. The sun's heat had nestled itself deep in our throats and we thought, perhaps, we'd stop for the night. The three of us pedaled across the one-lane highway and pulled into the gas station that sat just north of the intersection. Gary and Bob went inside as I wandered down the road looking for something resembling a town.

"I don't see anything worth staying for," I reported to the boys who sat snacking on orange juice and Fig Newtons. "There are a few closed-up buildings and I didn't see anyone around."

"Why don't we continue to Gila Bend?" Gary interjected pointing at the map that lay on the gas station's picnic table. "The dot's larger. It's got to be a bigger town and a better chance of finding a place for the night. It's only four o'clock. We should be able to cover the thirty miles." Bob and I nodded.

"The store has plenty of good snacks, Michelle," Gary added. "Why don't you grab something before we move on?"

"I'm not hungry," I said, our eyes meeting and holding for just a second. He said nothing more as he pushed the last Fig Newton whole into his mouth.

Back on the dust-covered road the late afternoon sun rested quietly to our rights, baking the already crisp landscape we cycled through. We fell into single file with Bob leading, me in the back, and Gary in the middle keeping an eye on us both. Conversation ceased and as the afternoon wore on the distance between us lengthened.

It was this time of day, long after lunch, when my body slowed. Not the natural slowing that's expected after six to eight hours of cycling, but a shutting down of a body that has nothing left, a body that needed food. I tried to ignore the tingling in my fingertips and the slight shake of my legs. I cursed what I believed was lack of training, lack of fitness, and my body's weakness. It was a hunger I did not know. I pedaled slowly, deliberately pushing and pulling to keep moving forward.

When we arrived at Gila Bend, I wanted nothing more than to lie in the grass and not move. To close my eyes and shut out the daunting task of bathing, setting up camp, and finding dinner. Sensing my uselessness, Gary sat me down and instructed me to eat crackers. "You should have eaten at the gas station," he said. "You really have to stop skipping those snacks."

Irritation swelled at his suggestion that I eat. I did not feel hungry; I had not felt hungry at the gas station. But the thought of salt made my mouth salivate. I ate the crackers. I felt better.

In my junior year in high school, the alarm clock went off at exactly 6 A.M. I reached over, turned it off, and moved my hands directly to my abdomen. Feeling my hipbones protruding and the amount of belly resting between them, I determined if it was going to be a good day. An empty feeling sometimes shot through my ribcage. Hunger pains. They calmed me, told me I hadn't overeaten the night before. I rose, showered, and prepared for the school day. Before leaving my room to join my mom in the kitchen, I opened my diary and reviewed yesterday's food:

Breakfast: exactly one-half bran muffin and tea

Lunch: a banana, an apple

Dinner: a small green salad with carrot shavings, low-fat

French dressing; two pieces wheat toast with low-fat American cheese

After dinner: a cup of nonfat, sugar-free hot chocolate

Total: 725 calories.

Not bad I thought and closed the diary. No workout though. Walking toward the kitchen, I planned the day's food in my head: eight hundred is fine as long as I can work out. Better keep breakfast light just in case the workout does not fit in.

"You really should finish that," Gary commented, nodding toward my half-eaten sandwich. The three of us were having lunch at a café in Rock Port, Arizona, just off Highway 17. It was a log cabin sort of place with wooden walls and wooden tables. We'd cycled from Sun City that morning and hoped to cover the ninety miles that day to Camp Verde.

"I'm full. Still full from the big breakfast," I responded fingering the other half of my grilled cheese sandwich and looking at him across the red-and white-checkered tablecloth. I thought about the three large pancakes I'd eaten that morning, with maple syrup and no butter. It was a lot of food. It had to be enough.

"We've been climbing all morning and if I'm reading this map correctly, we continue to climb. You'll need the calories." He paused and looked at me. "Look, if you do the math it makes more sense. Say we burn about eight calories a minute. If we ride for eight hours that's 480 minutes which makes our caloric need at around four thousand. That's not calculating climbs, or more hours in the saddle, or our bodies' energy needs beyond riding. So, we're looking at four to five thousand calories a day."

Four to five thousand calories a day.

"How about dessert?" the waitress inquired as she cleared our lunch plates.

"We have the best homemade pies around: apple, blueberry, chocolate. You name it." She looked at us inquisitively with a smile that suggested she'd be shocked if we passed on the pies.

Bob and Gary ordered immediately and they simultaneously said: "Michelle." I calculated quickly. I'd planned on having dessert

after the 100-mile day but never did. This could be it. Backlog, it
was fine. "Chocolate. I'll have chocolate."

One night during my senior year in high school, I made it home
from a date just before my midnight curfew. After gently shaking
my mother's shoulder and whispering I'm home, I made my way to
the kitchen and quietly opened the cabinet. Peanut butter, marshmallow cream and graham crackers on the table in front of me,
spoon in hand, I ate. Slowly at first, looking over my shoulder. Then
more quickly. I stopped tasting the creamy smoothness of the peanut
butter and the sweet sugar of the marshmallow. My chest tighten-
ing, my hands unsteady, I continued to chew and swallow until my
breath became short and the tears began to flow. I became aware of
what I was doing. Aware of its absurdity, but unaware of what was
behind it. Panicked because I could neither stop eating or resolve to
eat. I went to the bathroom and tried to rid myself of the anxiety
and guilt.

Over the years I willed it away, wished it gone as many times as
I had wished for a new stomach. The wishing seemed effective as
in college I no longer shook in the presence of buffets. I did not
cancel dates because I felt fat. I stopped writing down every morsel
that went into my mouth and every workout completed. Those
journals were thrown away in one of my many resolutions that food
and exercise would no longer control my life. But the change was
really because I had become conscious of what I was doing.

Consciousness led to guilt, guilt that others were hungry and I
was concerned about the size of my waist. Embarrassment, shame,
and common sense kept me from repeating what I had done in high
school, but it did nothing to dispel the definitions of body, food,
and self I had written. They became the unconscious caloric calcu-
lation of what was on my plate. The tears that appeared when I
stood naked in front of the mirror. The façade I put up when dining with friends while my roommate wondered why I rarely
cooked dinner. The belief buried deep in my belly that I would be
a stronger, better person in a different body. By the time I packed

my panniers I had become skilled at hiding such things. I appeared
to most as any other weight-conscious women, a little cautious of
French fries, but nothing more. I held on to what was different, con-
vincing myself that it meant I was fine. I ignored the weight in my
belly, the ache of truth, denied it so much that at times I actually
believed it was gone.

I didn't think of these things as we finished our dessert and began
the long climb to Camp Verde. I was proud I'd eaten the pie.
Triumphant, as if it proved that food was no longer an issue. Head
down, I pedaled quietly and took my place at the end of our cara-
van. Few cars passed us as we cycled on the wide shoulder. The sun
moved closer to the earth and I did not feel like riding. I thought
of the many rides Gary and I took back in San Francisco.

The times near the end of the day when he looked pleased with
the accomplishment and I quietly smiled, not wanting him to know
I hated riding at that moment, hated feeling wiped out. Yet I loved
being out there too, loved the feeling of freedom and release, and
had trusted that at some point my body would adapt.

I looked up and noticed that the boys were ahead of me.
Disappointment and the familiar tingle ran through me. It was as if
my blood flowed faster but was not getting anywhere. I fought
against it and pedaled harder, thinking no, this is not happening.
How can it be? I just ate, and dessert too.

A wave of nausea. Clammy sweat. I could no longer deny that
the shaking was back. That in reality, I wanted to simply sit. My slow
pedal soon became none and I stood, legs straddling the bike. Why
hadn't I felt hungry? How could it hit me so fast? I am eating.

I swung my leg over the bike and let it fall to the ground. I
dropped down next to it trying to comprehend what I was doing
wrong. I'm eating when I'm hungry, eating until I'm satisfied.
Aren't those the rules? But hunger was elusive to me. I hated feeling it, hated admitting I needed to eat. Hunger had come to mean
weakness, dependence. And I'd stopped acknowledging it long ago.

A warm wind passed over my clammy skin as cars passed by but
I did not look up at them. I sat, head down, crushed by the reality

that it was not over. Crushed because this was not who I wanted to be. I did what I had always done: tried to get out of my own skin. I looked up and down the highway as if it would offer some form of cover, some place I could squeeze into and leave my body on the side of the road. But out there, on that bike, I could not hide; I could not cloister myself at home or in an oversized shirt, pretending. The road exposed me and so I sat there and rested with it. After a short period of time, the boys returned, encouraged me back on my bike, and we moved on.

A few days later, we passed through Sedona on our way to Flagstaff, climbing out of rust-red desert and into tree-lined mountains. Each switchback put us in and out of the wind while revealing a larger expanse of rich forest and blue sky. The road was narrow and steep with no shoulder. The majority of my view became the continuous white line on the blacktop and I played a game of trying to keep my wheels on it. In this downward glance, my eyes also caught sight of the pushing and pulling of my legs. My calves, my thighs, and my hips worked in unison to move me up the mountain. I became aware of my belly and my back, of the sweat under my helmet, and the determination in my body. The regular exhale of my breath became louder and I smiled to myself awkwardly, embarrassed by the sudden presence of my body.

We left Arizona, crossed New Mexico, and settled in for the night in a small town that would put us over the Texas border the next day. Gary locked the hotel door and the three of us walked down the one main road. It was dark, only a few streetlights lined the road, and we hoped we'd find an open restaurant. A fast food and ice cream joint radiated bright fluorescent light; we walked in its direction. It reminded me of Frosty Burger, the place of my first job.

Bob and Gary ordered burgers and shakes. I ordered a grilled cheese sandwich and a real vanilla shake. We slid into the corner booth, spread our meal on paper wrappers, and pulled out the Texas map. We sat eating dinner, reviewing the map, and planning the next day's ride. All of us cleaned our plates.

As the miles shifted into days and Texas ranches became Tennessee hills and Tennessee hills became historical Pennsylvania, I too began to shift. I ate breakfast, lunch, and dinner. I ate snacks. I immersed myself in life's essentials: food, drink, shelter, and warmth. I thought about miles and inclines, flat tires and rain. I thought about the strength of my body and the strength of my spirit. I pedaled, grinding my history, its lessons, and the countless times I'd willed it gone into my muscles and joints, until they became a part of my fiber.

And somewhere in New York State, about two to three cycling days west of Syracuse, I sat contentedly outside a convenience store eating mini-donuts. My back rested against the standard bland beige color of the cement wall and I felt the heat of the sun on my already toasted face. I popped a donut, the white-powered kind that leaves white traces around your lips, into my mouth and washed it down with chocolate milk.

I imagine I must have been thinking about something at the time, but I can't remember what it could have been. Perhaps that we had a few days left of the two-and-a-half-month bicycle trip. Perhaps of the life I was moving to. Perhaps I thought about Bob who had left us in Virginia, and wondered if he'd gotten home O.K. Maybe I simply watched people come and go, buy gas and soda.

I do remember, though, watching Gary come out of the store with his own midmorning snack. He smiled as he walked toward me, glancing to check on our bikes before he sat with a satisfied sigh. I do remember that I did not think about where the donuts would rest on my body but that they would probably sustain me for the last twenty miles of the day. I remember thinking I was not ready to end the trip and that I wanted to keep moving. But it felt done, oddly enough, and I knew that.

I took another sip of milk and placed the container on the blacktop, closed my eyes, and turned my face to the sun.

I read somewhere that it takes time—months, sometimes years—for an experience to seep into the consciousness, for its lessons to be acknowledged. For me, it started five months after the end of the trip.

We were living in Syracuse, New York. It was December, and I stood staring out of the window above the kitchen sink. The garage door ground open and I heard the splash of tires as they passed on the wet road in front of the house. Behind me, the door opened and Gary walked in shaking off the cold with a short, sharp shiver.

"How about going out to dinner?" he inquired, my eyes catching his in the window's reflection.

Never in the mood to cook and hungry at the mention of food I responded, "Sure." He headed back out the garage door. I grabbed my coat and bent to tie my shoes. As I stood up, I stopped, conscious that I had responded instinctively. It struck me then: It had been months since I last calculated the day's food intake before deciding on dinner. Months since I had looked at the clock to see if it was time to eat. I couldn't remember the last time I felt my belly to assess its size. And just now, standing in the kitchen, I had not been thinking about my next meal or struggling with whether or not I deserved it.

I stood in the kitchen amazed. Amazed that these things I had done unfailingly for the past ten years were gone. Amazed, too, that I had not noticed until now. For just a second I was unsure of what to do, then relief took over. It went through me, lightened me, and I felt empty. Not the empty of something missing, but the empty of something finished. There was room now, room in me for something more.

Over time I came to see that after time on the road, and on the side of the road, I stepped out of my way and let my body lead. I came to see that what I craved was not food or a better body, but my own approval. I still prefer to shower before eating, and sometimes I brush me teeth in order to rid my mouth, and therefore my mind, of food. And there are moments, but just moments, when it is difficult to eat and difficult not to. I suspect this residue will be with me a long time, but I don't mind. It reminds me that my mind is filled with thoughts of work, family, career, and travel. It reminds me that I have a choice and of the richness of life.

"Are you coming?" Gary shouted from the garage.

I grabbed my wallet, pushed open the door, and climbed into the car.

"Do you want to go to Tully's or should we just head for pizza?" he asked as we drove toward town.

"We had that great pasta dish at Tully's, didn't we?" I said, talking more to myself than to him.

"Yeah, I think so."

"O.K., then," I said, "Let's go to Tully's."

Intent on traveling as soon as possible, Michelle Hamilton chose her college based on its study abroad program. While studying in England, she traveled to Paris, Amsterdam, and Russia. She's been hooked ever since and has found her way across the United States, to India, Nepal, China, and Taiwan. She lives and works in San Francisco.

DIANE RIGDA

Sourtoe Cocktail

She should have had a few drinks
before having this one.

I OPTIMISTICALLY REASONED THAT MY GLASS MUST BE DISTORTING
the toe, hovering in my whiskey sour, making it look even bigger
and more gray and shriveled. Soon the deed would be over but not
before the severed human toe touched my lips. I only hoped that
the cut end, with a bone and tendons trailing out, wouldn't be the
part to make contact.

Carlos, a friend of our hosts in Whitehorse, Yukon, mildly advised
that if we get to Dawson City, we must try the Sourtoe Cocktail. He
described the outrageous drink in his humble, soft voice. I just
couldn't believe it. "A real human toe?" I asked. That can't be.

"Yes, the big toe, and you're not supposed to swallow it, eh,"
Carlos added.

"Come on…" I insisted.

Carlos explained the history and mechanics of the Sourtoe
telling me, "Captain Dick is the eccentric gentleman in charge of
carrying out the tradition." He lost at least two prized toes in the
last few years to misguided, already inebriated partakers who swallowed the sickly frill.

Unlike south of the border where the drinker is encouraged to
swallow the tequila worm, the Yukon only requires a touch of the

lips to this drink's reusable accessory. Where the tequila worm merely resides in the bottle, this toe intimately occupies your glass. Worms may be easier to come by than toes but "Captain Dick always managed to replenish his supply of severed big toes." The thought made me shudder and curl my own tender digits. I was intrigued and couldn't get this toe cocktail out of my mind.

By road we followed the fourth largest river in the world, the Yukon, to Dawson City, a small town of 2,200. My travel mates and I walked on the raised, wooden plank sidewalks, seeking out the official man with the toe. We found the Downtown Hotel as Carlos had described. I climbed the wooden stairs onto a wrap-around veranda and pushed through the swinging wood-slat half-doors, like a gun-slinging cowboy with something to say. It was after midnight so the crowd was thin.

I approached the bar armed with my crazy request, "I'll have a Sourtoe Cocktail." The bartender shouted to a lone guy sitting in the corner with a briefcase, that she had a toe customer. He was packing to go but looked up to see the four of us. "Only one of us will be having the toe treatment," I assured him as he looked at his watch.

"Get a drink and come on over," he advised. I debated between Bailey's Irish Cream and a whiskey sour. "I don't think Bailey's would be a good choice for the Sourtoe," the bartender cringed. "The cream will cling to the toe," she persuaded delicately, respecting that I might still lose my nerve.

I ordered a whiskey sour and with that the bartender handed me a glass of ice water "for the toe," she informed. I walked over to Captain Dick but the man introduced himself as First Mate Cory, shaking my hand. He had replaced Captain Dick a few years back. Don't know what happened to Dick or his toes.

My squeamish friends seated themselves nearby. Cory tapped a tiny wooden coffin against the tabletop while I settled down to follow my destiny. I paid him a five-dollar supplement for the toe service. With his fingers, he lifted a grayish-white, withered body part out of the salt in which it was packed. He rinsed the toe in the ice water and dropped it into my drink.

❋

> I know a prospector who lost his toe;
> Froze it in the deadly cold and snow.
> He ran rum with a fast dog team
> (From the Yukon to Alaska it would seem).
> Deadly gangrene soon set in.
> He cut it off, his life to win.
> To remember the gruesome task he'd done,
> He pickled it in a jar of o.p. rum!

It wasn't hairy, but its former owner had neglected it, permitting an immortal callus. The large toenail had mottled shades of dead and the sight of it dispelled any doubt that this could be a hoax. "Where did you get this one?" I asked, regretting my question even before I finished the sentence. I could not bring myself to study the cut end too carefully, as if averting my eyes from something forbidden. Indeed.

> The fearsome thing was in a darkened jar.
> As Bartender Pete slapped it on the bar.
> As he pulled it out with silver tong
> A gasp went up from the gathered throng....

"Someone had bad circulation and had to have his leg off, eh," Cory said.

"Is the owner of this toe still alive?" I queried, not knowing which could be worse.

"Yep, he's still around," Cory cheerily volunteered.

Enough questions. I just wanted to get on with it, but not being a big drinker nor one who downs shots, I sipped my drink while Cory and my friends looked on. My whiskey sour tasted salty and I would not, under any circumstances, think about those toe juices leeching into my drink.

> As he grasped the frosted glass with shaking hand
> A mighty hush fell over the gathered band.
> The glass he raised to quaking lip

And with a shudder took a mighty sip.
He gagged, then with a gasp and frown,
He tilted back the glass and drank it down.

I took a deep breath, fleetingly distanced myself from the whole scene, then tipped back my glass. I felt what must have been the toe-nail click against my teeth. It all happened in a blur. I swallowed the last of my whiskey sour.

First Mate Cory took the glass to retrieve the toe and announced that I'd done it. I remember hearing cheers from my friends and the few stragglers left in the bar. It was after midnight but the sun had not yet set. It was time for me to get to bed and merely dream about the strangeness of the Yukon.

I have a card that I carry in my wallet near my driver's license. First Mate Cory filled in my name before handing me the membership/donor card and encouraged me to sign it. I am number 2,077 since 1995 to partake in this little known Yukon ritual. If ever I am in an accident, my own modest big toe can bask in the limelight, touching the lips of thousands—many more than while it's been attached to my foot.

If you go and are willing to try:
Downtown Hotel Bar
Corner of 2nd Avenue
and Queen
Dawson City, Yukon,
CANADA YOB 1G0
Ph: (867) 993-5346
Fax: (867) 993-5076
Supplement: $5 Canadian

If you're willing to contribute...
Send toe (big toe only) to:
Sourtoe Cocktail
P.O. Box 780
Dawson City, Yukon,
CANADA YOB 1G0

Diane Rigda traveled solo for twenty-one months in the Middle East and Africa. The anonymous poem in the story came from the certificate she received on that fateful night. She lives in San Francisco, California.

A Curry to Die For

The flavor will stay with you forever.

I ONCE WAS A GOURMET TRAVELER. FOR ME, TO SHARE THE GROW-ing, preparing, serving, and eating rituals of a country was to over-come any language barrier, to create intimacy and understanding. I still believe this, but when I met the curry makers of Makala I was also forced to realize the extent of my enslavement to taste and the powerful social consequences of our search for the rare, sublime, ultimate taste.

It happened in Kota Baharu on Malaysia's west coast, near the Thai boarder. Here I spent the days exploring temples, markets, and seaside villages and at night I ate my way through the superb food stalls that set up in the inner-city car park at dusk each evening. I indulged in spicy roast chickens, stuffed squid, satays, curries, *laksas*, and chili noodles enjoying the exotic smells, festive sounds, and smiling faces that became familiar as the other aficionado accepted me as one of their own.

It was here that I heard of a curry so special that you would never find it in markets or restaurants. It is made to order and only served at special feasts and weddings—a curry of celebration. I was told it was very expensive and the taste so exquisite that once you had eaten it you would long for it forever. I learned that this special curry was made in a nearby village, and that I could reach it by a two-hour trip up the broad, yellow river that twisted through the city.

The next morning I found my way to the ferry wharf, the gourmet tourist on a quest. The heat was a little less oppressive on the river. I enjoyed a semaphoric conversation with fellow passengers returning to their villages and luxuriated in the rich, fetid smell of rot seeping from the riot of vegetation that foamed like blue-green thunderheads over the riverbanks. Eventually we came to a rickety wooden pier behind which, through dense forest, a small gathering of tin roofs marked the village.

The ferryman gestured to me to disembark and made signs that I hoped meant he would return to collect me in two hours. It was with some trepidation that I watched the little boat disappear into the rainforest. I didn't know if I had the right place and there was no one around to ask. Perhaps, with the language barrier, I hadn't been clear about my destination. I was alone in the jungle in the most fundamental of Muslim states in Malaysia and I suddenly felt very vulnerable. Still, the tantalizing thought of the ultimate curry fortified me and, calling on the help of Saint Catherine Hepburn of the African Queen, I struck off in search of my own Holy Grail.

There is no such thing as curry powder in India. Rather, the term "curry" refers to the overall spicing of the dish. Various combinations of spices result in a sweet, salty, bitter, astringent, sour, or pungent flavor—the six flavors around which Indian meals are based. These spices not only flavor and color the food, they are also used to stimulate appetite or digestion. Foods are also spiced depending on the season. I was in India during the winter, so I ate more "heating" foods, prepared with stimulating spices such as cloves, cinnamon, peppercorns, chilies, ginger, and cumin.

—Deborah Fryer, "Food of the Gods"

The Malayan house is timber clad with a corrugated iron roof, and raised on stilts with open verandas to catch the breeze. In the city, and along the highways, they are usually surrounded by brilliant bursts of tropical flowers and neat little garden plots. But here the houses pressed in on each other as if herded together by the encroaching wall of forest.

Since there was no one to ask for directions, I began to wander along the bare earth track between the homes hoping I was not giving offense by trampling over private property. The place seemed deserted. The only sign of life was a mangy dog following me at a distance.

In the eerie silence, the village closed in on me the farther I walked. Imperceptibly, the purpose and form of the buildings changed from homes to work sites until I found myself at an intersection in a maze of tin sheds. I chose a path at random and turned to go down it.

"Phist! Phist!"

I turned around to see a gnarled old woman urgently beckoning me.

"Curry? You want to see curry? Come! Come!"

Her spine was so twisted she was almost bent double but, once she was sure I was following her, she set off at such a pace that I almost had to run to keep up.

The sun was now bouncing off the corrugated tin walls, intensifying the tropical heat and glare. I began to feel like Alice chasing the white rabbit.

So intent was I on not losing my gnomic guide as she led me farther and farther into the metal labyrinth that I found myself in the curry factory before I'd even realized it. I darted around what I thought to be another corner and was suddenly lost in a hot thick haze of pungent smoke. The heat hit me with a full body punch, taking my breath away. The smoke stung my eyes and burned my throat. But it was the aroma that made me go weak at the knees. I stood still, savoring the smell. A complex mix of memories assailed me, filling my mouth with desire.

Slowly I regained my breath. My eyes adjusted to the gloom. I was in a large tin shed about thirty by forty feet. Shafts of light fell from three-foot-wide strip of chicken wire between the roof and the walls, dimly illuminating the tableau before me.

Spaced evenly throughout the shed were five giant woks, each set into the top of a small circular stone well. Beneath them, small fires burned a dull red in the haze. Women moved around them, specters in the smoke. Those closest to me had stopped what they were doing and were watching me. I became aware of whispering, a background crackle of burning kindling, and dull muted coughing. Suddenly someone laughed and the women resumed their labor.

My guide had disappeared so I moved over to the group nearest me. Four women circled the wok and as I approached they shuffled around to clear a space for me. Though the smell was exquisitely evocative, I could only identify roast beef. The mix was too rich, too subtle to identify any one ingredient over another. And there were scents I'd never experienced before.

Years of cooking just this one curry had permeated everything in the building with its exotic incense—the woks, the stone fire-places, the timber wall supports, the bare earth floor, and the women themselves. The smells of the past were an essence giving further body to the scent of this current brew.

One of the women scooped a pinch of the mixture into her mouth indicating that I should do the same. The texture was that of fine shreds of beef, dry-fried yet moist. The initial taste was almost mellow but full-bodied, like aged wine, with a subtle hint of wood smoke.

The secondary taste exploded like a Dvorjac symphony of flavors—loud, exciting, extending, teasing, eluding, rich, and complex. And finally—the aftertaste of longing.

It was all I could do not to abandon myself to gluttony, to grab great handfuls, and stuff my mouth full of it. I frightened myself with an absurd desire to smear it on my body, rub it into my skin so that I would always taste it, smell of it. My greed must have shown in my eyes for the women were bent forward, watching me closely with their empty ladles at the ready. I was, of course, not their first victim, and its possible they were preparing to restrain me should I lose control in my intoxication. I smiled, they smiled.

One of the women handed me a ladle about the size of a small shovel and indicated another woman who showed me how to use it to turn the giant mound, which must only ever graze the hot wok. The fire was low and wide and I had to bend at an awkward angle to scrape, shovel, and toss the heavy mass. We worked in unison, almost like a dance, to the sounds of kindling and coughing, the rhythmic swish of metal against metal and the soft plop of ladles unburdened with a flick of the wrist.

Within moments I was perspiring heavily. Sweat poured from my face as I leaned over the wok, dripping into it. Embarrassed and ashamed, I pulled back. But the women laughed. One pointed to her face. She too was sweating profusely. Another exaggeratedly wiped her brow and flicked her hand into the wok. I was shocked, and again the women laughed.

We resumed our heave and toss but I was too slow and the worker reclaimed her tool just in time to rescue the little pile of beef drying in front of me.

I stepped back and felt someone tugging at my skirt; a disembodied hand reached up out of the smoke to offer me a glass of cold tea. Squatting down I found myself in a clear space below the bank of smoke. Here, in filtered light at the level of the fires, I could see the next shift of workers, including the grinning hag who'd been my guide. They were squatting, sipping drinks, waiting to relieve those working above us.

An attractive young woman caught my eye and, indicating that I should follow her, led me outside into clear air.

"Women's work!" I said wryly as I bent to wipe my face on my skirt.

"Yes, women's work," she responded, mirroring my irony.

"It's a good thing we're the weaker sex," I said in admiration of their labor. She laughed.

Her name was Sumata and she had been working over the smoking vats for two years. She had grown up in the village but left to study for a business degree in Kuala Lumpur. Though she had majored in international trade and spoke English and German fluently, she had been unable to find work in her field. After many years of fruitless effort to change her fate, she had returned home to follow in the footsteps of her mother and the women who had gone before her.

While I am sensitive to the possibility of giving offense by offering advice, I felt a moral outrage at the suffering of these women.

"There must be lots of lung disease," I noted.

"Yes, we die of lung disease," she replied, looking away. "It is an occupational hazard."

"Chimneys would make a big difference."

"The curry needs the smoke."

"God, my back hurts. Isn't there some way to make the labor easier?"

"Hand stirring for so long is what makes our curry rare. And our sweat adds flavor to the meat."

Then she fixed me with her eyes.

"Our suffering is the marinade. This beef costs lives and you can taste it. People know and respect this. And pay well."

Then she laughed, "It is as close to cannibalism as you can get without a body to dispose of."

She walked me back to the jetty. Before we left she ducked back into the factory and returned with a small package that she gave me as the ferry prepared to pull away from the wharf.

"After tasting our curry some people are never again satisfied. All other food is lacking. I'm sorry you have tasted it. If you use this sparingly, perhaps it will help. When it is gone you may come back."

Sumata was right. The curry has jaded my palate. While I still break bread with the locals when I travel, the pleasure of gourmet travel seems to have faded.

Margi O'Connell-Hood is a community activist who ate her way through the fauna and flora of Australia, India, and Asia until a visit to a village in Malaysia made her question her obsession with food. She makes her living as a consultant to community organizations and her pleasure is blue water cruising. She lives in Queensland, Australia.

* * *

Purifying Spirits

*If she can recall, it was quite
a farewell party.*

I HAVE NOW PROVED CONCLUSIVELY THAT ONE PAIN DOES INDEED cancel out another; today I awoke with such an unprecedented hangover that this afternoon's dreaded departure from Pokhara meant nothing as compared with the activities of that personal Goddess of Destruction who seemed to be residing in my head.

In the course of a not abstemious life, I have only once before had a hangover—at the age of twenty, after drinking a half-bottle of the cheapest Spanish brandy—but obviously it was the mingling of chang and rakshi that did the damage. Kessang and the Khamba community of Pokhara had invited me to a 6 P.M. Tibetan farewell party at The Annapurna, and a Pardi Gurkha friend had invited me to a 9 P.M. Nepalese farewell party at a Thakkholi eating-house in the village—and having gone to both parties and drunk multi-racially I can't reasonably complain about the consequences.

The weather surpassed itself yesterday; at 4:30 P.M., after a day of heavy rain, Pokhara was subjected to a cloudburst that made the worst of the monsoon downpours look merely damp. This lasted for a whole terrifying hour, before stopping abruptly, as though a dam had been closed. Then we set out for The Annapurna, and my dog Tashi had to be carried all the way; at no point on the track was the furiously tearing water below my waist and at one stage it rose to neck-level and I had to swim to higher ground, gripping Tashi's scruff with one hand. Perhaps after all it was fortunate that I spent the evening pickled in alcohol: otherwise I might have awakened with pneumonia instead of a hangover.

When Tibetans give a party it is nothing less than a banquet. At first, because of the party to come, I tried to back-pedal when offered solid refreshment, but everything was so delicious that self-control became impossible—and would in any case have been impolite when such an effort had been made for the occasion. By the time I stood up from the meal at 8:30 I could scarcely walk; and some of my fellow guests were quite frankly dozing off with their heads on the table.

The Thakkholi eating-house was scrupulously clean, as Thakkholi homes almost always are, and the ochre walls and floor glowed warmly by the light of twisting flames that came leaping out of a hole in the ground in one corner—rather as though we were on the edge of a baby volcano. There were ten of us officially present for the meal—but innumerable others drifted in and out of the background shadows—and we all sat cross-legged in a circle, on little squares of Tibetan carpeting. Luckily the main meal was not served until 11 o'clock, though we were nibbling incessantly at various tidbits as we swilled the rawest of raw *rakshi*, ordered specially by my host from his village. He claimed that it was the most potent alcohol obtainable in Nepal (where no alcohol is exactly impotent) and today I am prepared to endorse this.

All the food was served on brilliantly burnished brass dishes of varying sizes—from minute ones for the hors d'oeuvres to circular trays for the rice—and our "nibblings" in fact amounted to quite a meal. We began with tiny strips of perfectly braised wild-goat meat—among the tastiest savories I have ever eaten—followed by fried sardine-like fish from the lake, followed by two hard-boiled eggs apiece, followed by one fried egg, followed by an omelet containing intolerably hot chopped peppers that compelled me to spit it out with more haste than good manners. And all the time we sipped steadily at *rakshi*, more *rakshi*, and still more *rakshi* until I felt as though a bonfire were burning in my guts—but by then I had passed the point of no return.

The main course consisted of a gigantic mound of rice, with curried vegetables and *dhal*. As it was being served, the local prostitute wandered in, hoping for a customer at the end of our revels; but she could see at a glance that after this party no one would be in a fit state to patronize her, so she immediately dropped her professional manner and settled down merely to be sociable. I have always thought her the best-looking woman in the village; she has fine-cut Aryan features, fair skin, and glossy, jet hair. By firelight she seemed quite beautiful—until one noticed that brittle unhappiness and unwomanliness which disfigures even the loveliest of her sisters in every country of the world. From her nose hung an enormous circular gold ornament, which compelled her to smoke her countless cigarettes through the corner of her mouth, and her clothes were ragged and filthy—though of such good quality that one suspected them of having been acquired as payment for favors received. One could see that this addition to the party displeased the Thakkholi proprietress—though it was only when her own attractive sixteen-year-old daughter began to talk to the gate-crasher that an indirect protest was made, sharply ordering the girl to bed.

I cannot pretend to know at what time the party ended; but when two swaying neighbors escorted me home and pushed me up the ladder I was quite unable to distinguish one end of my sleeping bag from the other—so I merely collapsed on top of it.

The next few hours were not restful; in the midst of sundry nightmares I awoke once, and for some moments remained firmly convinced that I was no longer a human being but one of Jupiter's satellites—a singularly disquieting delusion, possibly exclusive to *rakshi*. And today my condition resembled a serious illness rather than a hangover—indeed I have never had any illness from natural causes that felt even half so serious.

Pokhara airstrip chose the occasion to break all its own records for "erraticism." Though I had been requested to report at 9:30 for a 10:00 A.M. flight, our plane did not depart until 4:30 P.M. However, I was indifferent to this; it could not have mattered to me where I was, or for how long, or why. I sat in The Annapurna, wrapped in a cocoon of malaise and misery, with my fellow-revelers—none of them looking too robust—and we drank cup after cup of heavily salted black coffee, which is reputed to counteract the worst effect of *rakshi* poisoning, and our long silences were broken only by staccato comments on how very dreadful we felt.

Dervla Murphy is an Irish travel writer who enjoys seeing the world from the seat of a bicycle. She is the author of sixteen books, including Transylvania and Beyond: A Travel Memoir, Full Tilt: Ireland to India with a Bicycle, South from Limpopo: Travels Through South Africa, *and* The Waiting Land: A Spell in Nepal, *from which this story was excerpted.*

PART FIVE

ONE LAST BITE

LAURIE GOUGH

Fruits of Paradise

One taste is all it takes.

LAUDI AND I DISCOVER A GROVE OF WILD MANDARIN TREES PREG-
nant with juicy fat oranges dripping low to the ground. He climbs
the trees and throws them down to me. We can't stop eating them.
They're too full of sweetness. We eat, laugh, chase each other, and
squish open oranges into each other's faces. A tree close by bears
X-rated fruit that shocks me. It's red, fleshy, moist, and has no skin.
I pull one off and taste it like I've never tasted anything else. Inside
my mouth is an explosion of all that's forbidden, all that's sweet and
sour at the same time, and as I swallow it, it comes to me that nature
folds secrets into out-of-the-way places. We could live together on
this island of his forever. But I forget we're in a grove of wild man-
darins way up high, where life is lighter, where the world below is
a faded dream.

*Laurie Gough is a writer, teacher, and traveler whose work has appeared
in national newspapers, magazines, and in numerous anthologies. This was
excerpted from* Kite Strings of the Southern Cross: A Woman's Travel
Odyssey, *which won a Foreword Book of the Year silver medal and was a
Thomas Cook/Daily Telegraph Travel Book Award finalist. She lives in
Guelph, Ontario.*

Recommended Reading

Allende, Isabel. *Aphrodite: A Memoir of the Senses*. New York: HarperCollins, 1998.

Allison, Dorothy. *Trash*. Ithaca, NY: Firebrand, 1989.

Avakain, Arlene Voski. *Through the Kitchen Window: Women Explore the Intimate Meanings of Food and Cooking*. Boston: Beacon Press, 1998.

Banerji, Chitrita. *Food and Life in Bengal*. Columbia, Montana: South Asia Books, 1991.

Braider, Carol. *The Grammar of Cooking*. New York: Holt, Rinehart & Winston, 1974.

Brillant-Savarin, Jean Anthelme. M.F.K. Fisher (translator). *The Physiology of Taste: Or Meditations on Transcendental Gastronomy*. Washington, DC: Counterpoint Press, 2000.

Chamberlain, Samuel. *Clementine in the Kitchen*. New York: Modern Library, 2001.

Colwin, Laurie. *Home Cooking: A Writer in the Kitchen*. New York: Alfred A. Knopf, 1988.

Colwin, Laurie. *More Home Cooking: A Writer Returns to the Kitchen*. New York: HarperCollins, 1993.

David, Elizabeth. *An Omelette and a Glass of Wine*. New York: Viking Penguin, 1984.

Drinkwater, Carol. *The Olive Farm: A Memoir of Life, Love and Olive Oil in Southern France*. Woodstock, NY: Overlook Press, 2001.

Esquival, Laura. *Like Water for Chocolate: A Novel*. New York: Anchor Books, 1994.

Fisher, M.F.K. *The Art of Eating*. Saint Paul, Minn.: Hungry Minds, 1990.

Fisher, M.F.K. *As They Were*. New York: Vintage Press, 1983.

Fisher, M.F.K. *The Gastronomical Me*. San Francisco: Northpoint Press, 1989.

Fisher, M.F.K. *Long Ago in France: The Years in Dijon*. New York: Touchstone, 1992.

Gage, Fran. *Bread & Chocolate: My Food Life in San Francisco*. Seattle: Sasquatch, 1999.

Gough, Laurie. *Kite Strings of the Southern Cross: A Woman's Travel Odyssey*. San Francisco: Travelers' Tales, 1999.

Johnston, Tracy. *Shooting the Boh: A Woman's Voyage Down the Wildest River in Borneo*. New York: Vintage Departures, 1992.

Loomis, Susan Herrmann. *On Rue Tatin: Living and Cooking in a French Town*. New York: Broadway, 2001.

Lust, Teresa. *Pass the Polenta: And Other Writings from the Kitchen*. New York: Ballantine, 1999.

Mayes, Frances. *Bella Tuscany: The Sweet Life in Italy*. New York: Broadway, 1999.

Mayes, Frances. *Under the Tuscan Sun: At Home in Italy*. New York: Broadway, 1997.

Moore, Judith. *Never Eat Your Heart Out*. New York: Farrar Straus Giroux, 1997.

Murphy, Dervla. *The Waiting Land: A Spell in Nepal*. Woodstock, NY: Overlook Press, 1987.

Reichl, Ruth. *Comfort Me with Apples: More Adventures at the Table*. New York: Random House, 2001.

Reichl, Ruth. *Tender at the Bone: Growing Up at the Table*. London: Ebury Press; New York: Broadway, 1998.

Shapiro, Laura. *Perfection Salad: Women and Cooking at the Turn of the Century*. New York: Modern Library, 2001.

Storace, Patricia. *Dinner with Persephone: Travels in Greece*. New York: Vintage, 1997.

Tannahill, Reay. *Food in History*. New York: Crown Publishers, 1988.

Toklas, Alice B. *The Alice B. Toklas Cookbook*. New York: HarperPerennial, 1984.

Winegardner, Mark, editor. *We Are What We Ate: 24 Memories of Food*. San Diego, Calif.: Harcourt Brace, 1998.

Index of Contributors

Acknowledgments

Thanks to the folks at Travelers' Tales for all of their hard work bringing this book to fruition, and for all of the incredible potluck meals we've shared. Special thanks to Larry Habegger for being a wonderful colleague and golfing companion, and to Susan Brady, for her friendship, dedication to detail, and Thai curry soup. Additional gratitude goes to: Tanya Pearlman, Tara Weaver, Kathy Meengs, Krista Holmstrom, Jennifer Leo, the O'Reilly's, and Michele Wetherbee.

To my family, who taught me that the best times together are spent around a table—talking, laughing, and eating. I am grateful for all of the unconditional love from: Barbara and William Bach; David, Laura, Aaron, and Noah Bach; Amy, Steve, Joshua, Jacob, Daniel, and Jessica Volin. I must also especially recognize my mother's matzo ball soup, potato latkes, and chopped liver. To my extended family—who thankfully also like to eat: Jane Thacker, Stacy Thacker, Penni Dougherty, Lee Ashworth, and Marshall Klein.

With a full glass of sweet dessert wine I toast my friends, whom I've shared countless extraordinary meals and ample good times with: Kim Arnone, Kevin Bentley, Andie Bourguet, Jeff Campbell, Phil Hahn, Laura Harger, Daniel Jason, Sally Kim, Karen Levine, Rachel Longan, Jenn Nannini, Gena Rickon, Inge Schilperoord, Erica Smith, Tacy Trowbridge, Deanna Quinones, Beth Weber, and Sue White. And to Robin Helbling and Leisha Fry, who initiated our supper club, although I still cannot figure out how me bringing you dinner once a month makes it a club.

And to Kara Thacker, who adds a dash of spice to my life and is always willing to share whatever's on her plate. I look forward to sitting down to many more meals with you, both at home and abroad.

"I Was Really Very Hungry" by M.F.K. Fisher excerpted from *As They Were* by M.F.K. Fisher. Copyright © 1955 by M.F.K. Fisher. Used by permission of Alfred A. Knopf, a division of Random House, Inc., and Lescher & Lescher, Ltd.
"Waiting for *Gözleme*" by Pier Roberts reprinted by permission of the author.

Selection from *Kite Strings of the Southern Cross: A Woman's Travel Odyssey* by Laurie Gough reprinted by permission of Travelers' Tales, Inc. and Turnstone Press. Copyright © 1999 by Laurie Gough. Published in Canada as *Island of the Human Heart*.

Selection from "Life in a Chilean Kitchen" by Heidi Schmaltz copyright © 2001 by Heidi Schmaltz.

Selection from "Lost in Spain" by Lucy McCauley published with permission of the author. Copyright © 2001 by Lucy McCauley.

Selection from "My Surreal Meals" by Kimberly Green published with permission of the author. Copyright © 2001 by Kimberly Green.

Selection from "The Pain of Chocolate" by Mary V. Davidson published with permission of the author. Copyright © 2001 by Mary V. Davidson.

Selection from "Sashimi Anyone?" by Laura Peterson published with permission of the author. Copyright © 2001 by Laura Peterson.

Selection from *Shooting the Boh: A Woman's Voyage Down the Wildest River in Borneo* by Tracy Johnston reprinted by permission of Vintage Books, a division of Random House, Inc. Copyright © 1992 by Tracy Johnston.

Selection from "Street Food" by Joan Aragone published with permission of the author. Copyright © 2001 by Joan Aragone.

Selection from "A Taste of Childhood" by Lisa Bach published with permission of the author. Copyright © 2001 by Lisa Bach.

Selection from "The Ties that Bind" by Susan Brady published with permission of the author. Copyright © 2001 by Susan Brady.

Selection from "A Walk in the Annapurnas" by Virginia Barton Brownback published with permission of the author. Copyright © 1987 by Virginia Barton Brownback.

Selection from "When a *Cucina* Says Yes" by Iyna Bort Caruso published with permission of the author. Copyright © 2001 by Iyna Bort Caruso.

Selection from "Yankee Pot Roast" by Helen Curley published with permission of the author. Copyright © 2001 by Helen Curley.

About the Editor

Lisa Bach is a freelance writer and editor with a Master's Degree in literature and more than ten years experience in book publishing. She is the editor of *365 Travel: A Daily Book of Journeys, Meditations, and Adventures*. She has eaten her way through more than twenty countries, but having just bought a home in Oakland, California, she will be spending more time with her luggage unpacked, in the kitchen cooking on her old Wedgewood stove. Visit www.HerForkintheRoad.com for more culinary information and gastronomical adventures.

TRAVELERS' TALES
THE SOUL OF TRAVEL

Footsteps Series

THE SWORD OF HEAVEN

A Five Continent Odyssey to Save the World
By Mikkel Aaland
ISBN 1-885-211-44-9
$24.00 (cloth)
"Few books capture the soul of the road like *The Sword of Heaven*, a sharp-edged, beautifully rendered memoir that will inspire anyone." —Phil Cousineau, author of *The Art of Pilgrimage*

TAKE ME WITH YOU

A Round-the-World Journey to Invite a Stranger Home
By Brad Newsham
ISBN 1-885-211-51-1
$24.00 (cloth)
"Newsham is an ideal guide. His journey, at heart, is into humanity." —Pico Iyer, author of *Video Night in Kathmandu*

LAST TROUT IN VENICE
The Far-Flung Escapades of an Accidental Adventurer
By Doug Lansky
ISBN 1-885-211-63-5
$14.95
"Traveling with Doug Lansky might result in a considerably shortened life expectancy…but what a way to go. —Tony Wheeler, Lonely Planet Publications

ONE YEAR OFF

Leaving It All Behind for a Round-the-World Journey with Our Children
By David Elliot Cohen
ISBN 1-885-211-65-1
$14.95
A once-in-a-lifetime adventure generously shared.

KITE STRINGS OF THE SOUTHERN CROSS

A Woman's Travel Odyssey
By Laurie Gough
ISBN 1-885-211-54-6
$14.95

—★★★—

ForeWord Silver Medal Winner
— *Travel Book of the Year*

STORM

A Motorcycle Journey of Love, Endurance, and Transformation
By Allen Noren
ISBN 1-885-211-45-7
$24.00 (cloth)

—★★★—

ForeWord Gold Medal Winner
— *Travel Book of the Year*

THE WAY OF THE WANDERER

Discover Your True Self Through Travel
By David Yeadon
ISBN 1-885-211-60-0
$14.95
Experience transformation through travel with this delightful, illustrated collection by award-winning author David Yeadon.

THE FIRE NEVER DIES

One Man's Raucous Romp Down the Road of Food, Passion, and Adventure
By Richard Sterling
ISBN 1-885-211-70-8
$14.95
"Sterling's writing is like spit-fire, foursquare and jazzy with crackle.…"
—*Kirkus Reviews*

Travelers' Tales Classics

THE ROYAL ROAD TO ROMANCE
By Richard Halliburton
ISBN 1-885-211-53-8
$14.95
"Laughing at hardships, dreaming of beauty, ardent for adventure, Halliburton has managed to sing into the pages of this glorious book his own exultant spirit of youth and freedom."
— *Chicago Post*

UNBEATEN TRACKS IN JAPAN
By Isabella L. Bird
ISBN 1-885-211-57-0
$14.95
Isabella Bird was one of the most adventurous women travelers of the 19th century with journeys to Tibet, Canada, Korea, Turkey, Hawaii, and Japan. A fascinating read for anyone interested in women's travel, spirituality, and Asian culture.

THE RIVERS RAN EAST
By Leonard Clark
ISBN 1-885-211-66-X
$16.95
Clark is the original Indiana Jones, relaying a breathtaking account of his search for the legendary El Dorado gold in the Amazon.

Europe

TUSCANY
True Stories
Edited by James O'Reilly, & Tara Austen Weaver
ISBN 1-885-211-68-6
$16.95
Journey into the heart of one of the most beloved regions on earth, the rolling hills and ancient cities of Tuscany.

GREECE
True Stories of Life on the Road
Edited by Larry Habegger, Sean O'Reilly & Brian Alexander
ISBN 1-885-211-52-X
$17.95
"This is the stuff memories can be duplicated from."
— *Foreign Service Journal*

IRELAND
True Stories of Life on the Emerald Isle
Edited by James O'Reilly, Larry Habegger & Sean O'Reilly
ISBN 1-885-211-46-5
$17.95

— ★ ★ ★ —

ForeWord Bronze Medal Winner
— *Travel Book of the Year*

FRANCE
True Stories of Life on the Road
Edited by James O'Reilly, Larry Habegger & Sean O'Reilly
ISBN 1-885-211-02-3
$17.95
The French passion for life bursts forth from every page, featuring stories by Peter Mayle, M.F.K. Fisher, Ina Caro, Jan Morris, Jon Krakauer and many more.

PARIS
True Stories of Life on the Road
Edited by James O'Reilly, Larry Habegger & Sean O'Reilly
ISBN 1-885-211-10-4
$17.95
"If Paris is the main dish, here is a rich and fascinat-ing assortment of hors d'oeuvres."
—Peter Mayle, author of *A Year in Provence*

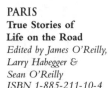

ITALY (Updated)
**True Stories of
Life on the Road**
*Edited by Anne Calcagno
Introduction by Jan Morris*
ISBN 1-885-211-72-4
$18.95

— ★ ★ —

*ForeWord Silver
Medal Winner—
Travel Book of the Year*

SPAIN
**True Stories of
Life on the Road**
Edited by Lucy McCauley
ISBN 1-885-211-07-4
$17.95

"A superb, eclectic collection that reeks wonderfully of gazpacho and paella, and resonates with sounds of heel-clicking and flamenco singing."
—Barnaby Conrad, author of *Matador*

Asia/Pacific

AUSTRALIA
**True Stories of
Life Down Under**
Edited by Larry Habegger
ISBN 1-885-211-40-6
$17.95

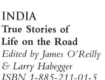

Explore Australia with authors Paul Theroux, Robyn Davidson, Bruce Chatwin, Pico Iyer, Tim Cahill, and many more.

JAPAN
**True Stories of
Life on the Road**
*Edited by Donald W.
George & Amy
Greimann Carlson*
ISBN 1-885-211-04-X
$17.95

"Readers of this entertaining anthology will be better equipped to plot a rewarding course through the marvelously bewildering, bewitching cultural landscape of Japan." — *Time* (Asia)

INDIA
**True Stories of
Life on the Road**
*Edited by James O'Reilly
& Larry Habegger*
ISBN 1-885-211-01-5
$17.95

"The Travelers' Tales series should become required reading for anyone visiting a foreign country." — *St. Petersburg Times*

NEPAL
**True Stories of
Life on the Road**
*Edited by Rajendra
S. Khadka*
ISBN 1-885-211-14-7
$17.95

"If there's one thing traditional guidebooks lack, it's the really juicy travel information, the personal stories about back alleys and brief encounters. This series fills this gap." — *Diversion*

THAILAND
**True Stories of
Life on the Road**
*Edited by James O'Reilly
& Larry Habegger*
ISBN 1-885-211-05-8
$17.95

— ★ ★ —

*Winner of the Lowell
Thomas Award for Best
Travel Book—Society of
American Travel Writers*

HONG KONG
**True Stories of
Life on the Road**
*Edited by James O'Reilly,
Larry Habegger &
Sean O'Reilly*
ISBN 1-885-211-03-1
$17.95

"*Travelers' Tales Hong Kong* will delight the senses and heighten the sensibilities, whether you are an armchair traveler or an old China hand."
—*Profiles*

The Americas

AMERICA
True Stories of
Life on the Road
Edited by Fred Setterberg
ISBN 1-885-211-28-7
$19.95
"Look no further.
This book is America."
—David Yeadon, author
of *Lost Worlds*

HAWAI'I
True Stories of
the Island Spirit
Edited by Rick &
Marcie Carroll
ISBN 1-885-211-35-X
$17.95
"Travelers' Tales aims to
convey the excitement of
voyaging through exotic

territory with a vivacity that guidebooks can
only hint at."—*Millenium Whole Earth Catalog*

GRAND CANYON
True Stories of Life
Below the Rim
Edited by Sean O'Reilly,
James O'Reilly &
Larry Habegger
ISBN 1-885-211-34-1
$17.95
"As entertaining and
informative for the arm-
chair traveler as it is for veteran river-rats and
canyoneers." —*The Bloomsbury Review*

SAN FRANCISCO
True Stories of
Life on the Road
Edited by James O'Reilly,
Larry Habegger &
Sean O'Reilly
ISBN 1-885-211-08-2
$17.95
"Like spying on
the natives."

—*San Francisco Chronicle*

AMERICAN SOUTHWEST
True Stories
Edited by Sean O'Reilly
and James O'Reilly
ISBN 1-885-211-58-9
$17.95
Put on your boots, saddle
up, and explore the
American Southwest with
Terry Tempest Williams, Edward Abbey,
Barbara Kingsolver, Alex Shoumatoff,
and more.

MEXICO (Updated)
True Stories
Edited by James O'Reilly
& Larry Habegger
ISBN 1-885-211-59-7
$17.95

— ★ ★ ★ —
One of the Year's Best
Travel Books on Mexico
—The New York
Times

BRAZIL
True Stories of
Life on the Road
Edited by Annette Haddad
& Scott Doggett
Introduction by Alex
Shoumatoff
ISBN 1-885-211-11-2
$17.95

— ★ ★ ★ —
Benjamin Franklin
Silver Award Winner

CUBA
True Stories
Edited by Tom Miller
ISBN 1-885-211-62-7
$17.95
A collection that sheds
light on the dazzling
mixture that is Cuba, in
all its fervent, heartstopping
complexity.

Women's Travel

A WOMAN'S PASSION FOR TRAVEL

More True Stories from A Woman's World
Edited by Marybeth Bond
& Pamela Michael
ISBN 1-885-211-36-8
$17.95

"A diverse and gripping series of stories!" —Arlene Blum, author of *Annapurna: A Woman's Place*

A WOMAN'S WORLD

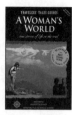

True Stories of Life on the Road
Edited by Marybeth Bond
Introduction by
Dervla Murphy
ISBN 1-885-211-06-6
$17.95

— ✦✦✦ —

*Winner of the Lowell Thomas Award for Best Travel Book —
Society of American Travel Writers*

WOMEN IN THE WILD

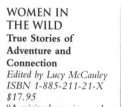

True Stories of Adventure and Connection
Edited by Lucy McCauley
ISBN 1-885-211-21-X
$17.95

"A spiritual, moving, and totally female book to take you around the world and back." —*Mademoiselle*

A MOTHER'S WORLD

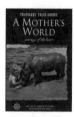

Journeys of the Heart
Edited by Marybeth Bond
& Pamela Michael
ISBN 1-885-211-26-0
$14.95

"These stories remind us that motherhood is one of the great unifying forces in the world" —*San Francisco Examiner*

Spiritual Travel

A WOMAN'S PATH

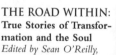

Women's Best Spiritual Travel Writing
Edited by Lucy McCauley,
Amy G. Carlson &
Jennifer Leo
ISBN 1-885-211-48-1
$16.95

"A sensitive exploration of women's lives that have been unexpectedly and spiritually touched by travel experiences.... Highly recommended."
—*Library Journal*

THE ULTIMATE JOURNEY

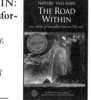

Inspiring Stories of Living and Dying
James O'Reilly, Sean
O'Reilly & Richard Sterling
ISBN 1-885-211-38-4
$17.95

"A glorious collection of writings about the ultimate adventure. A book to keep by one's bedside—and close to one's heart." —Philip Zaleski, editor, *The Best Spiritual Writing series*

THE ROAD WITHIN:

True Stories of Transformation and the Soul
Edited by Sean O'Reilly,
James O'Reilly &
Tim O'Reilly
ISBN 1-885-211-19-8
$17.95

— ✦✦✦ —

*Best Spiritual Book—Independent
Publisher's Book Award*

PILGRIMAGE

Adventures of the Spirit
Edited by Sean O'Reilly
& James O'Reilly
Introduction by
Phil Cousineau
ISBN 1-885-211-56-2
$16.95

— ✦✦✦ —

*ForeWord Silver Medal Winner
—Travel Book of the Year*

Adventure

TESTOSTERONE PLANET
True Stories from a Man's World
Edited by Sean O'Reilly, Larry Habegger & James O'Reilly
ISBN 1-885-211-43-0
$17.95
Thrills and laughter with

some of today's best writers: Sebastian Junger, Tim Cahill, Bill Bryson, Jon Krakauer, and Frank McCourt.

DANGER!
True Stories of Trouble and Survival
Edited by James O'Reilly, Larry Habegger & Sean O'Reilly
ISBN 1-885-211-32-5
$17.95
"Exciting…for those who

enjoy living on the edge or prefer to read the survival stories of others, this is a good pick." —*Library Journal*

Travel Humor

NOT SO FUNNY WHEN IT HAPPENED
The Best of Travel Humor and Misadventure
Edited by Tim Cahill
ISBN 1-885-211-55-4
$12.95
Laugh with Bill Bryson, Dave Barry, Anne Lamott, Adair Lara, Doug Lansky, and many more.

THERE'S NO TOILET PAPER…ON THE ROAD LESS TRAVELED
The Best of Travel Humor and Misadventure
Edited by Doug Lansky
ISBN 1-885-211-27-9
$12.95

Humor Book of the Year —Independent Publisher's Book Award

ForeWord Gold Medal Winner—Humor Book of the Year

Food

THE ADVENTURE OF FOOD
True Stories of Eating Everything
Edited by Richard Sterling
ISBN 1-885-211-37-6
$17.95
"These stories are bound to whet appetites for more than food."
—*Publishers Weekly*

FOOD
A Taste of the Road
Edited by Richard Sterling Introduction by Margo True
ISBN 1-885-211-09-0
$17.95

Silver Medal Winner of the Lowell Thomas Award for Best Travel Book—Society of American Travel Writers

HER FORK IN THE ROAD
Women Celebrate Food and Travel
Edited by Lisa Bach
ISBN 1-885-211-71-6
$16.95
A savory sampling of stories by some of the best writers in and out of the food and travel fields.

Special Interest

365 TRAVEL
**A Daily Book of
Journeys, Meditations,
and Adventures**
Edited by Lisa Bach
ISBN 1-885-211-67-8
$14.95
An illuminating collection
of travel wisdom and ad-

ventures that reminds us all
of the lessons we learn while on the road.

THE GIFT
OF RIVERS
**True Stories of
Life on the Water**
*Edited by Pamela Michael
Introduction by Robert Hass*
ISBN 1-885-211-42-2
$14.95

"*The Gift of Rivers* is a
soulful compendium of wonderful stories that
illuminate, educate, inspire, and delight. One
cannot read this compelling anthology without
coming away in awe of the strong hold rivers
exert on human imagination and history."
                    —David Brower, Chairman
                        of Earth Island Institute

FAMILY TRAVEL
**The Farther You Go,
the Closer You Get**
Edited by Laura Manske
ISBN 1-885-211-33-3
$17.95
"This is family travel at its
finest." —*Working Mother*

LOVE & ROMANCE
**True Stories of
Passion on the Road**
*Edited by Judith Babcock
Wylie*
ISBN 1-885-211-18-X
$17.95
"A wonderful book to
read by a crackling fire."
            —*Romantic Traveling*

THE GIFT
OF BIRDS
**True Encounters
with Avian Spirits**
*Edited by Larry Habegger
& Amy G. Carlson*
ISBN 1-885-211-41-4
$17.95
"These are all wonderful,
entertaining stories offering
a *bird's-eye view!* of our avian friends."
                    —*Booklist*

A DOG'S WORLD
**True Stories of
Man's Best Friend
on the Road**
*Edited by Christine
Hunsicker*
ISBN 1-885-211-23-6
$12.95
This extraordinary
collection includes stories
by John Steinbeck, Helen Thayer, James
Herriot, Pico Iyer, and many others.
A must for any dog and travel lover.

THE GIFT OF TRAVEL
The Best of Travelers' Tales
*Edited by Larry Habegger, James O'Reilly
& Sean O'Reilly*
ISBN 1-885-211-25-2
$14.95
"Like gourmet chefs in a French market,
the editors of Travelers' Tales pick, sift, and
prod their way through the weighty shelves
of contemporary travel writing, creaming
off the very best."

                    —William Dalrymple, author of *City of Djinns*

Travel Advice

SHITTING PRETTY
How to Stay Clean and Healthy While Traveling
By Dr. Jane Wilson-Howarth
ISBN 1-885-211-47-3
$12.95

A light-hearted book about a serious subject for millions of travelers— staying healthy on the road—written by international health expert, Dr. Jane Wilson-Howarth.

THE FEARLESS SHOPPER
How to Get the Best Deals on the Planet
By Kathy Borrus
ISBN 1-885-211-39-2
$14.95

"Anyone who reads *The Fearless Shopper* will come away a smarter, more responsible shopper and a more curious, culturally attuned traveler."
—Jo Mancuso, *The Shopologist*

THE PENNY PINCHER'S PASSPORT TO LUXURY TRAVEL
The Art of Cultivating Preferred Customer Status
By Joel L. Widzer
ISBN 1-885-211-31-7
$12.95

World travel expert Joel Widzer shares his proven techniques on how to travel first class at discount prices, even if you're not a frequent flyer.

SAFETY AND SECURITY FOR WOMEN WHO TRAVEL
By Sheila Swan & Peter Laufer
ISBN 1-885-211-29-5
$12.95

A must for every woman traveler!

THE FEARLESS DINER
Travel Tips and Wisdom for Eating around the World
By Richard Sterling
ISBN 1-885-211-22-8
$7.95

Combines practical advice on foodstuffs, habits, & etiquette, with hilarious accounts of others' eating adventures.

GUTSY WOMEN
More Travel Tips and Wisdom for the Road
By Marybeth Bond
ISBN 1-885-211-61-9
$12.95

Second Edition—Packed with funny, instructive, and inspiring advice for women heading out to see the world.

GUTSY MAMAS:
Travel Tips and Wisdom for Mothers on the Road
By Marybeth Bond
ISBN 1-885-211-20-1
$7.95

A delightful guide for mothers traveling with their children—or without them!